BASEBALL

FOR EVERYONE

BASEBALL

FOR EVERYONE

A Treasury of Baseball Lore and Instruction for Fans and Players

JOE DiMAGGIO

Line Illustrations by
LENNY HOLLREISER

ADVISORY BOARD
OF BASEBALL EXPERTS

Carl Hubbell   Bill Dickey

Frankie Frisch   Art Fletcher

with a special chapter
"How to Score"
by Red Barber

FOREWORD BY PETER GOLENBOCK

McGraw-Hill
Camden, Maine • New York • Chicago • San Francisco •
Lisbon • London • Madrid • Mexico City • Milan • New
Delhi • San Juan • Seoul • Singapore • Sydney • Toronto

McGraw-Hill

A Division of The McGraw·Hill Companies

10 9 8 7 6 5 4 3 2 1

Library of Congress Cataloging-in-Publication Data
Di Maggio, Joe, 1914–
   Baseball for everyone / Joe DiMaggio.
     p.   cm.
Originally published: New York : Whittlesey House, 1948.
Includes index.
   ISBN 0-07-138798-6 (hardcover : alk. paper)
  1. Baseball. I. Title.
   GV867 .D5 2002
   796.357—DC21   2001008524

This book is printed on 55# Sebago by R.R. Donnelley

FOREWORD

Peter Golenbock

The late 1940s was a special era for baseball, an age of innocence in which beloved players cavorting in legendary ballparks were mythic figures to be worshipped by their adoring fans. The best had memorable nicknames like The Splendid Splinter, The Springfield Rifle, Lefty, Dixie, or Duke. With their private lives shielded by the sports media, the focus always was on what they did on the field, allowing the greatest players to become true heroes to adults and children alike.

During this post–World War II era, the athlete who came to represent the myth of the American dream most closely was the eighth of nine children born to a Sicilian fisherman who had emigrated to the San Francisco Bay area in search of a better life. The story was that because the boy got seasick, he spurned fishing on his father's boat to become the greatest center fielder in the history of the game. That youngster, of course, was Joe DiMaggio. At the time, if you were to ask any American of Italian descent who the three greatest Italians in history were, the answer would have been unanimous: Dante, Verdi, and DiMaggio.

For an athletic youngster growing up in the late 1940s, no experience could have matched that of being tutored in the fundamentals of baseball by Joseph Paul DiMaggio, The Yankee Clipper.

It would have been as if a young painter were mentored by Michelangelo, or a young composer schooled by Beethoven. By reading *Baseball for Everyone*, a book DiMaggio wrote in 1948 with the help of New York sportswriter Tom Meany, a youngster had a chance to learn the game from the man who three times was named Most Valuable Player in the American League; who hit in 56 straight games, a record so incredible it is unlikely ever to be broken; and who was a lifetime .325 hitter with such remarkable bat control that over his brilliant thirteen-year career he had only eight fewer home runs (361) than strikeouts (369), a feat, when you really think about it, that was even more amazing than his consecutive-game hitting streak.

DiMaggio carried 200 pounds on his 6-foot, 2-inch frame, but when he moved to catch a baseball on the field, he glided to the ball with uncommon grace. He was, moreover, an uncanny judge of fly balls. No matter where the ball was hit, it always seemed that he would be waiting there under it, pounding his fist into his glove as the ball descended toward him.

One time DiMaggio was standing behind the batting cage during practice. His Yankee teammate, John Lindell, hit a towering drive.

"Over the fence," shouted several teammates.

"Hit the fence," said DiMaggio. The ball hit the fence.

"I can judge a ball within five feet," said DiMaggio matter of factly.

What the kids in the stands knew about DiMaggio was that he had arrived in New York in 1936 and immediately helped lead the Yankees to four straight pennants. There were two more pennants in 1941 and 1942, and after a stint in the service, he returned, and the Yankees won again in 1947, 1949, 1950, and 1951. When he retired after the '51 season, DiMaggio had won ten pennants in thirteen seasons of play.

What the kids may not have known about their hero was that he was an uncompromising perfectionist who mercilessly drove himself and his teammates. No one, his teammates said, hated to lose as much as Joe. If the Yankees lost a ballgame, and he went oh for four, DiMaggio felt that he somehow had let the club down. It wasn't surprising that he developed severe ulcers.

No one played with more pride than The Great DiMaggio. Every game he strived to be the best player in the world. Perfection was his goal, and no one ever came closer.

Once he was asked why he pushed himself so hard on the field. He replied, "I always think there might be someone out there in the stands who has never seen me play."

DiMaggio produced his wondrous 56-game hit streak in 1941. That year a song was written about him called "Joltin' Joe DiMaggio." Part of the refrain went, "We want him on our side." When the recording was released, it climbed to number one on the Hit Parade. The next year Joe entered the Army Air Force and the Second World War, and didn't return to baseball until 1946, when he hit .290 despite bone chips in both heels and torn cartilege in his left knee. The experts were saying he was through. He began '47 on crutches and in his first game back hit a three-run home run. He played on with excruciating pain, leading the Yankees to a surprise pennant.

By the middle of '48 he didn't know which leg to limp on, but despite the ailments that year hit .320, with 39 home runs, and drove in 155 runs. Red Smith of the *New York Times*, the leading sports columnist of the time, wrote: "The Yankees have a guy named DiMaggio. Sometimes a fellow gets a little tired writing about DiMaggio. A fellow thinks, 'There must be some other ball player in the world worth mentioning.' But there isn't really, not worth mentioning in the same breath with DiMaggio."

This was the same year in which DiMaggio, the most famous man in America with the exception of perhaps President Harry Truman, wrote *Baseball for Everyone*. Journalist Gay Talese once wrote, "Gods don't write letters." DiMaggio was one God who had made an exception. He didn't just write a letter. He wrote a whole book.

In 1948, when this book was first published, fans got their visual sports fix by going to the movies and watching the newsreels prior to the feature. Television would not explode into America's consciousness until the fall of 1951, when millions of sets were sold to watch the National League playoffs between the Brooklyn Dodgers and the New York Giants, and the World Series between the Giants and DiMaggio's New York Yankees.

Radio provided the play-by-play, and fans had to use their imaginations to picture what was happening. Radio broadcasters were among the most visible sports messengers. Mel Allen, who sang out, "Going, going, gone," whenever DiMaggio or a teammate hit a home run, was known as The Voice of the Yankees. Red Barber, who contributes a chapter in this book explaining how to keep a scorecard, was the radio voice of the Brooklyn Dodgers.

Before television, magazines unified the country by bringing words and pictures to the masses. The public feasted on such weekly publications as *Life*, *Time*, *Colliers*, and the *Saturday Evening Post*. Newspapers brought the news of the day. Sports fans waited on street corners for the trucks to deliver the paper so they could read the most up-to-date account of the day's ballgame.

In New York City alone, a Yankee fan could read about his team in the *New York Times*, the *News*, the *Post*, the *Herald Tribune*, the *World-Telegram*, and the *Sun*. The *Long Island Press*, *Newsday*, and *Brooklyn Eagle* also had fine sportswriters.

With all this information available, fans had plenty of ammunition for the year-round discussions and arguments. The pastime of talking baseball developed into a fine art. Who was better: the Yankees' shortstop Phil Rizzuto or the Dodgers' shortstop Pee Wee Reese? Who was better: the Yankees catcher Yogi Berra or the Dodgers catcher Roy Campanella? The arguments were fierce. But there was no argument when it came to center field. No one—not Tris Speaker, not even younger brother Dom DiMaggio—was better than Joe.

It's been fifty years since Joe DiMaggio played baseball. Only a select few other players, such as Babe Ruth and Jackie Robinson, have ascended to an immortality like Joltin' Joe's. Those who saw him play never forget it.

Ernest Hemingway was one of his biggest fans. In 1952 Hemingway memorialized DiMaggio in the classic novella, *The Old Man and the Sea*. The old fisherman, while fighting a large sailfish for more than two days, muses about whether The Great DiMaggio would have continued to fight the fish as he was doing. The fisherman concludes that he would have "since he is young and strong. Also his father was a fisherman. But would the bone spur hurt him too much?" The fisherman answered himself aloud. "I do not know. I never had a bone spur." Joe's name also was conjured up in the hit Rogers and Hammerstein musical *South Pacific*, which arrived on Broadway in 1949. The song "Bloody Mary" likens daughter Liat's tender skin to Joe DiMaggio's baseball glove.

If a youngster read *Baseball for Everyone* and followed what Joe Di had to say about playing the outfield, the kid might not play with a glove as tender as DiMaggio's, but he at least would have learned the proper mechanics for playing the position.

And now, with the republication of this book, a new generation of youngsters will benefit from Joe's wisdom and insights, while an older generation will have the chance to revisit those wonderful years when DiMaggio patrolled center field and America itself seemed younger—a little innocent, a little awkward, a little brash—like a baseball player who knows he's good but doesn't yet take it for granted. What's so marvelous about this book is that DiMaggio's advice and tips about the game are as relevant today as they were then, because in fact, though the world has changed greatly, the game of baseball never really changes. Oh, the American League now has the designated-hitter rule, some of the stadiums have domes, and now a pitcher needs the split-fingered fastball, where in the past he would have thrown an occasional shineball or spitter, but the essentials of the game don't change from one generation to the next. The bases are still 90 feet apart, and the techniques of positional play remain the same. Coaches still enourage their young players to get in front of a ground ball and to catch a fly with both hands, even though most major leaguers don't do that anymore.

This book is not only filled with hundreds of valuable tips on how to play the game, but it tells young players and fans about the emotions of the game, the pressures and the difficulties, what a rookie feels, and what it takes to compete successfully.

The book is also a time capsule in a way, because the advice and anecdotes come from long-gone baseball legends such as Bill Terry, John McGraw, Joe McCarthy (DiMaggio's longtime manager), and even the great Ty Cobb, who runs true to form with his advice to youngsters in a slump: try to hit a line drive right back at the pitcher's hands. *Baseball for Everyone* is filled with pure baseball. DiMaggio's knowledge of the game and his reverence for it come through on every page.

In 1954, six years after publication of *Baseball for Everyone* and three years after his retirement in 1951, Joe DiMaggio went from sports star to international celebrity when he married film goddess Marilyn Monroe. The marriage would end in divorce after nine months, and Joe would spend the rest of his life pining for her, even after her tragic death in 1962. His unrequited love helped transform him from hero to legend, an icon of pop American culture and the dignified pitchman of Mr. Coffee ads. But to his fans, who never forgot him, he was always the Yankee Clipper. I remember attending an Old Timer's Game at Yankee Stadium in the early 1960s. The highlight of the day was getting to watch the retired Yankees play a two-inning exhibition before the regular ballgame.

I had never seen DiMaggio hit before. I was only five when he retired. In this game the silver-haired idol, who hadn't swung a bat in anger in perhaps a dozen years, strode to the plate, and wearing the familiar pinstriped uniform with the number 5 on the back, he swung and hit a long drive deep into the left field stands. The sold-out throng of more than 70,000 fans stood as one to cheer. When he crossed the plate, he tipped his cap. I cheered as loudly as anyone. I looked to my right, and next to me a grizzled baseball fan said reverentially, "He was the best that ever was." The man stood there looking up at the sky, with tears rolling down his face.

As the age of innocence disappeared with the Vietnam War, the songwriter Paul Simon wondered how our society had become so cynical. In his song "Mrs. Robinson," written for the movie *The Graduate*, he harkened back to a more innocent time when Joltin' Joe once again would be on his side. Don't we all.

PETER GOLENBOCK
St. Petersburg, Florida
December 2001

Peter Golenbock's many books about baseball and sports in America include *Dynasty: The New York Yankees, 1949–1964*; *Balls* (with Graig Nettles); *Bums: An Oral History of the Brooklyn Dodgers*; *Wild, High and Tight: The Life and Death of Billy Martin*; *The Bronx Zoo* (written with Sparky Lyle to explore Yankee owner George Steinbrenner's treatment of his players); *Personal Fouls* (about corruption in the North Carolina State basketball program under coach Jim Valvano); and *Amazin'*, an oral history of the Mets to be published in 2002.

ACKNOWLEDGMENT

Everyone who tries to play baseball or to teach it has to thank a lot of people for everything he knows. For everyone who is playing or teaching the game today is doing his work with the help of all the people who have been in baseball before him. Whenever anyone came up with a smart play or devised an effective piece of strategy, the smart men of the game were quick to pick it up, adapt it to their own uses, or pass it on to their own players or teammates. If anyone comes up with a good new wrinkle today, the smart men will have it on their ticket tomorrow. So if I thanked, by name, everyone whose influence on baseball has helped me learn whatever I know about the game, the list of names would be longer than this book itself, and it would include a lot of people I have never seen and who have never heard of me. It would have to include baseball men like John McGraw and Connie Mack, the people from whom they first learned baseball, and the people to whom they passed their knowledge on. It would have to include my own managers, like Lefty O'Doul, Joe McCarthy, and Bucky Harris; and my teammates and players on other teams; and kids who were up only a year when I was a rookie and said to me, "Take it easy," or "Relax"; and Spike Hennessy and Charley Graham, who signed me to the Seals; and Frank Venezia, who asked me to play on a Boys Club League team from our block in San Francisco. I also have to thank all the sports writers who have sat around and talked to me in Pullmans, restaurants, and hotel lobbies and told me things about baseball I probably never would have learned from anybody else. For this particular book I want to thank Tom Meany and Maron Simon, without whose cooperation it never would have been written.

JOE DIMAGGIO

Contents

1. BASEBALL FOR EVERYONE 1

2. SAND LOT AND SEMIPRO 17

3. THE MINORS 28

4. THE MAJORS 42

5. FIRST BASE 53

6. THE SECOND BASEMAN 68

7. THIRD BASE 83

8. THE SHORTSTOP 97

9. THE ART OF CATCHING 110

10. PLAYING THE OUTFIELD 124

11. HITTING 139

12. PITCHING PROCEDURE 154

13. BASE RUNNING 170

14. COACHING AND SIGNS 183

15. SLUMPS 194

HOW TO SCORE by Red Barber 205

INDEX 211

1: Baseball for Everyone

IF YOU live in the United States, the chances are good that you're a part of baseball. Man or woman, strong or frail, rich or poor, energetic or lazy, probably you play baseball now, used to play it or will grow up to play it, or you're a fan, following your team at the ball park or poring over the newspapers or hanging onto the radio for news of the sport.

There is no official figure on the number of persons who take part in baseball, either as players or fans, and there's not likely to be until the government gives the census takers an enormous extra chore. But this will give you an idea of the grip of the game on our country:

In 1947 there was a total attendance of approximately 20,000,000 at the games of the two major leagues and more than 40,000,000 in the fifty-two minors. This does not mean that 60,000,000 different persons saw professional-league baseball games, but that the turnstiles clicked that many times; and the total number of individuals who paid their way into the nation's ball parks was surely enormous, even if some of them saw every game in their home parks.

Add to the teams in organized professional baseball the thousands of teams, with tens of thousands of players and millions of spectators, in amateur and semipro—the high-school teams, the college teams, the Boys Club leagues, the playground teams, the pickup nines, and the sand lotters. American League Junior Baseball alone had 1,000,000 boys playing on 30,000 teams in 1947. This project, for amateurs under seventeen, is the largest supervised amateur athletic endeavor in America.

A National Recreation Association survey shows that in

1946, the most recent year for which figures are available, the 1,153 cities reported the operation of 4,323 municipal baseball diamonds. Of these cities only 499, operating a total of 2,181 diamonds, reported attendance figures; the attendance was 18,547,620, including players and spectators.

To learn how many actually were playing baseball on municipal diamonds, we have to go back to the National Recreation Association's 1941 figures, the latest available. These show that 435 cities with 2,066 municipal diamonds reported participation—7,527,035.

No matter how many different players this seven and a half million actually represents, all the figures that can be assembled on baseball just go to prove that it is one of the most popular undertakings in American life, embracing all types and all classes of people. One has only to look at a group of fans, whether in New York or Cleveland or Roan Rapids or Carbondale, to realize how universal is the game's appeal.

I believe that the major reason for the greatness of baseball is the blood kinship of its players and its fans in their devotion to the game. One of their chief bonds is their fascination for intimate information about every aspect of baseball. And the more they find out, the keener they become as performers or as fans.

The success of this book will be measured largely in the understanding of baseball which it promotes, in the improvement which it makes possible for aspiring young players, in the increased interest which it stimulates among followers of our national game.

In the Army, in the company for the first time since my boyhood of fellows who weren't in baseball as a profession, I was more aware of the public's avid quest for baseball knowledge. Almost every soldier, including WACs and nurses, even those who rarely saw a game, questioned me incessantly about baseball. They wanted to know about the game itself—what they wanted to know about individual performers was only about those individuals as parts of the game.

This hunger for information about baseball was made clear to me again when I spent a couple of weeks in a New York hospital early in 1947. Many of the visitors I had were people I'd never seen before—boys who played sand-lot or semipro ball, reporters from high-school papers, or just plain fans. All of them had questions about baseball, and their questions formed an invariable pattern: How is a certain play made? Why do you do it that way? What's it like in the majors? What are major-leaguers like? How do you get to be a good ballplayer?

This book proposes to answer such questions by taking a tour of baseball play from the time a youngster tries "one old cat" until he hangs up his glove as an old-timer and moves on to middle age. Although the game belongs to the fans, and they are as important a part of baseball as the players, I can give the answers only in terms of the player, which still will suffice because fans and players are so much alike.

True lovers of baseball will go to any lengths of inconvenience or discomfort to play a game or to see one. The youngster from a poor family, carrying his ragged glove in his belt all day in the hope that his newspaper route will lead past a sand-lot diamond and a few innings before dark, is the brother of the clerk inventing the death of a nonexistent aunt on opening day. The established athlete who conceals the aches of fractured ribs to play in a crucial game and the aging fan who risks apoplexy to root his favorites home in front are kith and kin.

Players comb the newspapers, magazines, and radio programs for baseball stories of any sort, even those tiny filler paragraphs about the eating habits of some obscure player whom they most likely will never know. Busher Joe Blow's ability to eat three pounds of haddock at one sitting is unimportant, but because he's baseball, it's news to us.

Of the same family is the baseball-fanatic newspaper editor who wandered back to his office one hectic night just as the paper was coming off the press. It was late in December; snow was on the ground; the World Series was three months deep in history, and the next training season was three months ahead. There wasn't a breath of baseball in the air.

The paper was brimming with interesting and important stories—an international crisis, a sensational gang killing, a shipping strike, an airline crash. The editor scanned each column with a professional eye as he flipped the pages over to the sports section.

"Good paper tonight, isn't it, Jim?" a colleague remarked.

"Lousy," he growled as he crumpled the paper into a ball and heaved it angrily at a wastebasket. "No baseball news!"

Nor is there any great difference between the partisanship of the fan rooting for his pleasure and the devotion of the professional playing for his pay. The fan is a fan of one team, usually for life. The player, because he cannot pick and choose his employer and because he may be sold or traded to another club at any moment, can support only one specific team at a time— the team which is employing him. But to that team's victory and to the skillful handling of every situation which each game presents, the baseball player, if he's worth the name, dedicates himself without reservation; and those are the very things for which the true fan cheers until his throat is raw and his palms are red.

There is often similarity even between the youngster's selection of his position in his earliest sand-lot game and the fan's choice of the club to which he may be partisan. Both frequently may stem from sentiment.

"I'm Christy Mathewson; watch this fadeaway!" screams a

youthful worshiper of the late great Giant pitcher as he races to the box and begins to heave the ball at the nearest receiver.

"I'm George Sisler!" yells a small boy who has acquired a hand-me-down first baseman's mitt, or "I'm Ty Cobb!" shouts a young disciple of the Georgia Peach as he dashes for the out-field.

And baseball is full of fans who have pledged their loyalty to a certain team merely because some well-remembered old-time star, long dead or retired from the game, once graced its roster.

Usually a fan's loyalty is hereditary, or his partiality is for his home-town team, or, if his city has more than one team, for the club that's based in his neighborhood. But I've known South Chicagoans who jeered the White Sox and North Siders who couldn't stand the Cubs. And in New York, so many residents of which were born in other towns, there are a million reasons for the choice.

The chief point of difference between the player and the fan seems to me to be the age at which their respective interests in baseball are stirred.

Fans become fans at any time of life, and through any sort of inspiration. There is a rabid Giant fan who never saw a game of baseball until he moved to New York from Little Rock at the age of twenty-one. He didn't know a soul in the biggest city on earth and was lonely as only a friendless person in New York can be. He was sick at missing the companionship of his own city and the familiar greetings he could exchange there a dozen times in every block.

One day he learned that the Giants' shortstop was a young man named Travis Jackson, who once had played for the Little Rock Travelers in the Southern Association. Although the lonely Arkansan knew nothing about baseball, this former player on his home-town team became a symbol of happier days. He began to be a regular customer at the Polo Grounds. He never met Jackson, never saw him more closely than from a grandstand seat, but to this day, established, prosperous, and as New York as Fifth Avenue, he remains a Giant fan.

There is an eminent New York business executive who regarded baseball as unworthy of his notice until the World Series of 1934, when he became fascinated by the nickname "Ducky Wucky," attached implausibly to Joe "Muscles" Medwick, the star outfielder of the St. Louis Cardinals.

"What kind of game is it that produces a weird nickname like that for a hard-boiled guy like Medwick?" he asked a friend. That night he flew to Detroit, paid a fabulous price for a ticket to the final Series game, and launched himself on an unflagging career of rooting for the Cards.

The player's interest, however, if he's really going anywhere in baseball, must be aroused in his boyhood. And if he has the ambition and the skill, nothing can keep him down.

Joe McCarthy, who managed us to six pennants and five world championships in my first seven years with the Yankees, used to say, "Every once in a while somebody will tell you the story of a fellow he knows who could have been a big-leaguer except that the scouts didn't give him a tumble, or else he didn't want to be a professional ballplayer. I say bunk! If the fellow didn't feel like playing ball professionally he wouldn't have made it anyway because his disposition would have been against him. But if he had the ability and the desire, nothing could have kept him from being a major-leaguer. Without meaning to be disrespectful in the least, I say it's like a boy who wants to become a priest. If he feels that he has the call for that vocation nothing can stop him—poverty, a late start in education, or anything else."

I doubt if there is any way to fix the average age at which

an American boy first gets his hands on a baseball with a curiosity about its true usage. I can't remember when I first picked up a ball and tried to throw or catch it.

But I think I can set the time for my first competitive attempts in baseball, elementary though they were. I believe I was about ten years old.

Boys, I think, usually start playing baseball through curiosity and a desire for imitation. They see some other boys throwing or batting a ball around and they want to try it too. Usually they begin competitively on a rocky lot in a game that's called "one old cat" or "one o' cat" or "one eye cat," the name depending on the locality. Regardless of the name, the game's simplicity is universal. The personnel can consist of as few as two players, a pitcher and a batter. One stone represents home plate, another first base. The batter stands at the plate, the pitcher heaves the ball at him, and he tries to bat it far enough to allow him to run to first and back. If he flies out or is tagged out he becomes the pitcher, and the pitcher comes to bat.

If they can round up a few more players an extra base or two may be added, and the fielders advance in rotation to their turn at bat, the pitcher first, then the first baseman, the second baseman, and so on. Some local rules let the player making a put-out on a fly ball come to bat at once.

Elementary though this may be, it's the beginning of baseball as a competitive game for most American boys and for boys in many other baseball-playing nations as well. They're usually nine or ten when they take up "one old cat." Presently they're choosing up sides, and by the time they're twelve some of them have nine-man teams of their own, and even uniforms.

Here trouble can start that can spoil at the outset a boy's chances of becoming a real baseball player. Youngsters, like too many of their elders, try to do too much in a hurry. When they start team play, boys should have sufficient supervision to ensure that their play is contained within the limits of their physical capacity.

Baseball is exactly the game we know today because of the quality of the ball and the fact that the bases are set 90 feet apart, and the pitcher's rubber is 60 feet 6 inches from home plate. These distances dictate the timing of plays, the speed of pitches, the breaks and leads taken by runners, the responses of batters, everything that comprises the game as we know it and play it today. If the bases were 80 feet or 100 feet apart, and the pitching distance 50 or 70 feet, it wouldn't be the same game, even though the rules and the motions were identical.

These distances are right for grown men and many teen-agers, but for boys under fifteen they should be cut down. The softball diamond, which sets the bases *55 feet* apart and the pitcher 43 feet from the plate, should suit itself ideally for boys ten to twelve years old. On such a layout the catcher, for instance, has only a *73*-foot throw to second, against *127 feet* on the regulation diamond.

The National Joint Rules Committee recommends for boys under sixteen a diamond with the bases 82 feet apart, the pitching distance 50 feet, and the distance from home to second 115 feet 11½ inches. I have watched a lot of boys' games and I'm inclined to go along with Bert V. Dunne, a real student of ball-players of grammar-school age, who recommends in his book *Play Ball, Son!* that bases be 81 feet apart, with a pitching distance of 53 feet and a throw from home to second of 112 feet 6 inches. Fifty feet from mound to plate, even at that age, seems to be putting too great a handicap on the batter, according to many boys I've questioned and my own judgment of boys' pitching stuff.

When boys are playing "one old cat" or pick-up games on

the corner or in the pasture, the size of the diamond usually requires little supervision. The young players soon adjust themselves to their own capacities. Almost instinctively they can gauge the distance from which the pitcher should throw to the batter, the spacing of the bases, and the depth at which the fielders should play.

But once a boy of twelve or thereabouts begins playing on a formal diamond, as a member of an organized team, some wise elder should keep an eye on the measurements. It is a matter of pride with every boy to feel that he can meet his colleagues on even terms in any competition. In a "show 'em" spirit he'll try to make the throw from deep short or from home to second, whatever the distance and regardless of the strain on his arm.

There is no known remedy for a strained arm, despite the many ways of suffering one.

"I used to be a good thrower before I threw my arm out" is one of the saddest of tales among ballplayers, and there is no surer way of "throwing your arm out" than attempting long throws that are beyond one's physical capacity. A child playing ball on a regulation diamond is meeting the same demands which would face a major-league center fielder if he had to stand against the fence all afternoon and try to reach home plate on the fly.

Far less dreadful than an arm thrown out but still a frequent consequence of playing on oversize diamonds in boyhood is the acquisition of bad playing habits to compensate for lack of physical capacity. These habits are not fatal but they may take valuable years to cure, and in the case of a professional ballplayer his professional life is too short to allow the waste of years.

If the distance from home plate to second base is too great for a catcher to make the throw with a normal single step, the boy most probably will pick up the habit of taking the second step. The extra step added by the catcher when he makes his throw means literally and exactly the subtraction of one step from the distance which the runner must cover when he races from first to second. In a tight ball game such a gift is too extravagant.

Harry Danning, a good catcher and a hard hitter, can testify to the costliness of that specific habit. Sometime in his youth Danning fell into the extra-step habit when he threw to second. There was nothing wrong with Danning's arm; he just took an extra step. He first reported to the Giants at a training camp in 1931, but it was five years before he became a regular catcher with the club, principally because he couldn't break the habit.

He went from the Giants to the minors for three years, and because he was a fine hitter his minor-league managers didn't spend much time correcting his throwing style. Moreover, in the minors his arm was strong enough to throw out a high percentage of runners, despite the extra step. In the majors he couldn't get rid of the step, so he spent two years on the bench until he corrected the flaw. Before he was through as a Giant he was a good thrower, taking a single step forward with his left foot and pouring the ball down to second. When I played against the Giants in the 1937 and 1938 World Series there wasn't a thing the matter with Harry's throwing. Yet it had cost him a couple of important years to break a bad habit, even though he had the expert guidance of such men as Pancho Snyder, then a coach and formerly a great Giant catcher.

The speed with which players spot the least fault in an opponent and take full advantage of it, the nearest possible approach to perfection that good baseball demands of its performers, the priceless time lost in correcting a youthfully acquired fault make it an obligation of those charged with the supervision of young players to know their game and to see to it that their charges pick up no mechanical flaws.

This chapter deals solely with the common-sense rules for starting out in baseball, rules for youngsters and for those charged with their supervision, whether those mentors be fathers, older brothers, or paid instructors. Direct hints and instructions for improvement of natural skills come later in the discussions of position play. There is a right way and there is a wrong way to start out in baseball, and the lad who starts the right way not only will have less to unlearn but will eliminate the risk of permanent injury.

Little can be done to increase a boy's speed, but there is one very simple means of preventing its reduction. Provide a youngster with comfortable, well-fitting shoes. He may want a uniform more, or a chest protector, or a mask, or a big-name-model bat or mitt, but his shoes are most important of all. See that they fit him.

The boy of twelve or fourteen doesn't need a twenty-five-dollar-pair of featherweight shoes of kangaroo leather such as the pros wear but he must have shoes that do not pinch, blister, or deform his feet. He spends far more time on the field than any professional in any single game, as much as five hours at a stretch. He's on the field hours before a game starts and long after it is finished. That's a century in a pair of uncomfortable shoes.

When I was a boy playing sand-lot or playground baseball in San Francisco we used to buy spikes in a sporting-goods store and have the neighborhood cobbler attach them to a pair of ordinary street shoes. Such makeshifts will still suffice if the spikes are mounted properly and if the shoes were comfortable in the first place. For those who can buy better footgear, many sporting-goods stores carry reasonably priced baseball shoes for youngsters which are durable enough to last out a season or until the boy outgrows them, if he gives them the care that they deserve. For instance, don't walk on hard pavement in spikes, as too many youngsters do.

There is another precaution that a young ballplayer must take to keep his feet in shape. He must be sure to wear a clean, dry pair of socks each day. Aside from personal cleanliness, there are loads of medical reasons why damp, soiled hose must be avoided.

Choice of position for a boy playing his first formal baseball can very well be governed by circumstances. Almost without exception the best ballplayer is the pitcher on any team of twelve- or fourteen-year-olds. The reason is that pitching appeals to him as the job that offers the most action. And if a boy can throw harder, hit farther, and run faster than his teammates, usually he will take what he wants as his just due. Even on high-school teams, and frequently in college, the pitcher will be found to be batting in the middle of the order, in the spots reserved traditionally and logically for sluggers, never in ninth place.

In faster baseball it will begin to be apparent that the role of pitcher calls for a specialist, and, important as the pitcher is, he frequently can't hit, run, or field skillfully. He's often awkward, and in fact the only athletic part of his anatomy is his pitching arm.

It's in the faster company that the all-around ballplayer begins to desert pitching, to go for shortstop if he's right-handed, to first base if he's left-handed. Perhaps through trial and error he will gravitate to the outfield, or to another infield position. The hardier souls, if they throw right-handed, may take up catching.

There is no reason for a player to remain at a particular position simply because it is the first one into which he drifted. If he has a sensible coach or manager he will be moved as soon as it becomes apparent that his talents are better utilized elsewhere. When the famous brother battery of Mort and Walker Cooper started out in boyhood in Missouri their current positions were reversed. Mort was then the catcher and Walker the pitcher.

In 1942, after the Cardinals had beaten the Yankees in the World Series, Walker pitched and Mort caught an exhibition game in Kansas City, just to show that they had not lost their old skills. Mort lost the game for his brother by letting a pitched ball get away from him, but the box score in the newspapers next morning read: "Losing pitcher—W. Cooper."

"What a joke!" Walker snorted when he read it. "You lost that game for me."

"Now you know how we pitchers feel about you catchers," Mort retorted.

The record books are full of the names of players who changed their positions as they matured. Augie Galan, the valuable National League outfielder, was originally an infielder. In the first professional game in which I ever played, for the the San Francisco Seals, I took Augie's place at shortstop.

Babe Ruth, as everyone knows, was a fine left-handed pitcher until Ed Barrow, then managing the Boston Red Sox, decided to use his big bat every day and turned him into an outfielder. The Babe, while he was at St. Mary's Institute for Boys, in Baltimore, was a perfect example of a pitcher as the best player on a youngsters' team.

Probably because it is so laborious, the job of catching is the most difficult in which to interest not only the twelve-year-old, but the big-leaguer as well. A catcher has a hard job, often thankless: he's baseball's blocking back. But there is rarely a good ball club without a good catcher, or a good football team without a good blocking back.

Yet catcher, of all baseball positions, is the first for which a youngster can determine if he has any special aptitude. There are players who came up to the majors as catchers and then were shifted to other positions. Mel Ott is a prize example. (The interchangeable Coopers had settled down to their current positions before they entered professional baseball.)

The only two I can recall who shifted to catcher after they had reached the majors are Moe Berg and Bobby Bragan, and Berg had done some catching as a schoolboy at Barrington High in Newark, New Jersey. Moe drifted from Brooklyn to the minors and joined the White Sox in 1927 as an infielder. In a game against Boston, Chicago's two regular catchers were injured. Moe volunteered to take on the pad and mask and on his first throw down to second he served notice that he was no clown behind the plate. The ball hit the base and stuck between the bag and the ground.

Bragan had played shortstop throughout his professional career and came up to the Phillies as a shortstop. Hans Lobert, the Phils' manager, acted on a hunch and converted him to catcher. The hunch paid off.

Finally, the Cardinals used outfielder Don Padgett as a catcher, but Padgett had caught for a time in the minors.

No young player should be in a rush to decide whether he's an infielder, an outfielder, a pitcher, or a catcher—yes, even a catcher, as the examples of Bragan, Berg, and Padgett prove.

Bucky Walters, who pitched Cincinnati to its only two pennants in almost thirty years, had three tries in the majors as an infielder before the late Jimmy Wilson, then managing the Phillies, used him on the mound. Back in the 1920's Bob Smith, a Braves infielder, decided to become a pitcher and stuck around for years. Johnny Cooney came to the Braves as a promising left-handed pitcher, injured his arm, and became one of the surest and smoothest outfielders the majors have seen.

If a player is left-handed he has an edge at pitching or at first base. If he's right-handed he has all the nine positions from which to choose, and though there may be a slight percentage against first base there have been many right-handed first basemen in the majors, and good ones, too.

The chief thing for players under sixteen to remember is that they're playing for fun, for healthy exercise, and to learn the basic principles of sound play. Almost invariably they will drift into the positions for which they are best suited. The advice of older players or qualified supervisors should be well heeded; and if they suggest a shift, take their advice. All of us, especially when we're young, are inclined to overestimate our abilities. Our teammates usually can appraise us more accurately than we ourselves can.

But for the boy who intends to make a career of baseball, even sixteen is not too young an age at which to begin to take serious inventory of certain special abilities. A principal one, except for pitchers and catchers, is speed of foot. A boy doesn't have to be a 10-second sprinter, but if he's slower than average, right now is the time for him to look on baseball as no more than a week-end diversion. The other essential is a strong throwing arm. Speed and strong arms are God-given attributes. No amount of practice or effort will develop them.

When Branch Rickey first organized the huge tryout camps of the Cardinals, the first time baseball ever put on a wholesale talent hunt among teen-agers, his scouts wasted no time separating the sheep from the goats. First they staged a series of sprints, which eliminated about a third of the youngsters who reported. Next they staged a throwing contest, which eliminated another third.

This system, not standard operating procedure at all major-league tryout camps, may seem harsh and arbitrary. One might ask, "What if a boy has a great arm but lacks speed? Or what if he runs like a streak but can't throw?" Branch Rickey and all the other elders of the game know from a world of experience that it takes both to make a major-leaguer, and it is a major-leaguer that they are looking for.

The odds against any player's becoming a major-leaguer are tremendous, just on the basis of the number of available jobs. There are millions of fellows playing baseball in this country today. There are only two major leagues, only sixteen major-league clubs, each with a player limit of twenty-five. This means that, no matter how many candidates there are, only 400, including the reserves, can be chosen at any one time.

But, as Joe McCarthy says, if a player has the skill plus the determination, he'll make the majors, no matter what the odds may be.

2: Sand Lot and Semipro

ONE OF the greatest thrills and one of the truest opportunities that comes to a young baseball player is his first invitation to play on a regular, organized team. It was certainly so with me, when an older boy in our San Francisco block asked me to join a Boys Club League team that he was organizing.

Any boy of fourteen or more who has a chance to play in an organized league—Junior American Legion, Sunday-school, or scholastic—should jump at the chance. It is his best possible opportunity to improve his play and his practical and theoretical knowledge of the game. For example, 113 American Leaguers and 91 National Leaguers of 1947 were former American Legion Junior Baseball players.

Playing in a league, he has equal opportunity with his fellows and has an excellent chance to judge his own capabilities. He plays against the same team several times and learns what makes for standout qualities in other players. He is in a position to study the performance of his betters at first hand.

Whether a player is a boy in his teens or an adult who has made the majors, he has room for improvement, and his three chief ways of learning better baseball are through good instruction, personal observation, and intelligent questions. In a league he can observe the good hitters, pitchers, and fielders, and compare their techniques with his own. He can see the good hitter bat against the good pitcher. He can watch the good pitcher work on the good hitter.

In a league he gets his first knowledge of the inexorable law of percentages. He discovers that it isn't just good luck that enables some hitters to get more hits, and some pitchers to pitch more winning games than others in similar spots.

In league play, too, instructions from the manager are more readily carried out, and tips from older teammates are more readily put to use, than in unorganized games.

In league play a certain pitcher may make a sucker out of a batter in one game, but the batter will have other opportunities during the course of a regular schedule to face him again, to study, and to solve his deliveries. In unorganized play the batter may never face that particular pitcher again.

Moreover, in a league a youngster is in constant association with other baseball players, whether they play no more than a couple of times a week. Even when they're not playing or practicing they'll travel together and they'll talk baseball most of the time. These constant conversations—clinics and post-mortems—are as helpful to a young baseball player as are chalk talks and skull sessions to a football squad.

Participation in organized athletics requires certain sacrifices of personal freedom. No one engaged in regular competition can disregard the demands of good physical condition. A part-time ballplayer must be more diligent in keeping himself in condition than one who plays the game daily. The fellow who plays ball every day plays himself into shape and stays there.

It is an absolute must of physical conditioning that every player take a sufficient warm-up before each game, that he never cut loose with his arm until he has played catch long enough to remove all the stiffness developed by the period of idleness before the game. The longer the layoff, the longer the warm-up.

Johnny Rigney, a good pitcher for the Chicago White Sox before the war and now an executive with that club, is off the active list today, at the age of only thirty-three years, because he ignored that precaution.

When the war came Rigney went into the Navy. He landed

on Guam one day to find a ball game scheduled between two teams of servicemen, with Johnny van der Meer, of double no-hit fame, pitching for one club. The sailors on the other team asked Rigney to pitch for them.

Rigney hadn't touched a ball in a couple of years and he was accustomed to getting his arm into shape through weeks of spring training. But he felt that he couldn't let his mates down and he warmed up as best he could. Intense pain in his arm forced him to quit the game after a few innings, and he was never able to do much pitching again. He went to Johns Hopkins Hospital in the winter of 1947 for an examination by surgeon George Bennett, who advised him that even an operation would not help, and that his pitching days were over.

Week-end baseball doesn't require rigorous exercises, such as team football demands. It does, however, necessitate a certain amount of daily exercise to assure the player that his muscles won't tighten up and hobble him with a Charley horse every time he gets into a game. In most cases plenty of walking during the week will be sufficient to keep the occasional player loose and supple for his Saturday or Sunday game.

An occasional game of catch will suffice to keep his arm and back muscles limber. And anyone aiming at a career as a professional baseball player should certainly have sense enough to get a good night's sleep every night and to eat regularly and moderately.

The few sacrifices required for the sake of good condition are not onerous, and if a profession in baseball is hoped for they are well worth while. Boys in other endeavors give up a lot of their social life to learn a trade at night school after work. If baseball is to be your trade, strict attention must be paid to the fundamentals. Obviously, physical conditioning is basic.

For the youngster playing semipro ball, the financial returns are apt to be pretty slim, especially at the outset. The pay roll is limited by the receipts, and it is the veteran regulars who get most of the money. This may seem unfair to the youngster, but he must remember that the veterans have been playing semipro ball for years and usually are at the peak of their skill; they form the nucleus of tried and proven players on whom the semipro club's owner or manager can depend year in, year out, while the youngster, with the opportunities of his whole career ahead of him, may be stopping over for just a little while.

I was fourteen years old when I received my first money for playing ball. It amounted to $8, and not even that was in cash, but an order for merchandise. And to get the $8 worth of merchandise I had to play through a whole season with my Boys Club League team and hit two home runs in the playoff game in which we won the championship.

At that, I fared better than Nick Etten, who later played first base on the Yankees for a couple of years. Etten lived in Chicago, on the South Side. One summer during high-school vacation, the manager of a traveling semipro club called up Nick's home and asked if he'd like to play a game over on the North Side. Flattered that somebody was offering actual cash for his baseball services, Etten readily assented.

The game wasn't played in an enclosed field and the gate receipts depended upon the generosity of the fans among whom the hat was passed. The money was then divided between the two teams and then among the members of each team. Etten's share came to exactly seventy-five cents!

"The next week this manager had the nerve to call me up again and ask me if I'd care to play another game for him," Etten later told me.

"I was still burned up over the seventy-five cents, so I said to him, 'What, go all the way across Chicago for six bits?' "

"His answer really floored me. 'You don't think you're worth any more, do you?' said the guy."

Today a boy capable of playing what is called "fast semipro" won't have to settle for small change. I don't suppose that in these days any semipro manager would dare offer a player less than $10 for a game. The standard minimum for playing semipro ball in any park where admission is charged is about $25 for a regular, with pitchers getting as much as $75. Top semipro players, of course, command proportionately more.

If a player is good enough for first-flight semipro ball he can easily command $100 a week during the baseball season. And this while working at his regular job in the meantime. Baseball thus can be a quite profitable sideline; semipro pay lures many youngsters away from other jobs. The profits explain why so many players in their late twenties and even late thirties hang on to semipro jobs.

It must be remembered, however, that strong semipro teams such as the Bushwicks in New York City, the Logan Squares in Chicago, the Lit Brothers team in Philadelphia, and others of similar caliber require a degree of skill sufficient to qualify a player for the middle-bracket minors, certainly as high as Class B and maybe as high as Class A. And if it is a big-leaguer a youngster wishes to be, he goes to the big leagues from the minors, not from the semipros.

Among the better semipro clubs the young player will meet veterans, quite often former major-leaguers, who can help him greatly with advice. Often the newcomer will have the chance to play against members of big-league teams in post-season exhibition games. Watch the big-leaguers carefully to learn what they have that gives them a steady living from baseball instead of merely a chance to pick up some money on the side.

The young player must be careful not to let occasional success in a good semipro competition give him an exaggerated sense of his own skill. Sometimes in semipro games against barnstorming major-leaguers he may tag a "name" pitcher for a real line drive or strike out a first-class hitter. For these barn-stormers their regular season—a long, exhausting six months—is over and frequently they've let down from their normal zeal to win.

The best place for a young player to get a true appraisal of his capabilities is at a tryout camp. Branch Rickey started these camps with an establishment at St. Joseph, Missouri, when he was trying to find players with which to stock his farm clubs. Since then they have expanded tremendously, and major-league clubs conduct them throughout the country the year around.

During the season they are conducted in the vicinity of the major-league cities, sometimes even in the major-league parks while the clubs are on the road. As winter approaches they are moved to the South and Southwest, and usually there are a few operating in Southern California in December and January.

Usually a club announces that a tryout camp will be operated in a near-by town for two or three days and invites all young-sters in the vicinity to come out for a trial, bringing their own equipment.

In Rickey's early camps a couple of scouts observed the play-ers and selected likely-looking material for assignment to clubs in the lower minor leagues. Scouts still conduct the camps today but now they double in brass as instructors.

Instruction in these camps is of enormous value to the young man who wishes to be a ballplayer. He benefits not merely from the experience of a veteran professional, but from a professional who has shown a special talent as an instructor. This is highly important, since not every man who can do a job well himself can tell others how to do it.

Furthermore, the instructors at these tryout camps have a vital interest in their jobs. Not only are they contributing to the development of better baseball, but it is a mark in their favor back in the home office each time a pupil from their camp can make good. They have as much interest in the progress of a boy from one of their camps as has a scout in a player whose signing he has recommended.

As to the quality of the players who are picked up in these tryout camps—two regulars who six years earlier had walked unheralded into a Dodger camp at San Mateo, California, helped bring the Brooklyn team into the 1947 World Series. They were Spider Jorgensen, third baseman, and catcher Bruce Edwards.

The best steer I can give a boy who shows baseball skill is to grab his glove and spikes and report to any major-league tryout camp operating in his locality. First and foremost, he cannot help learning *something*, even in the few days the camp is in session. Secondly, it gives him a chance to parade his wares before people who are looking for professional ballplayers.

My brother Dominic got his professional start from a tryout camp operated by the San Francisco Seals. Dom is short and wears glasses. These facts counted against him with scouts who looked him over when he played sand-lot ball. At the tryout camp, under the close scrutiny of several professional observers, he won the decision.

Tryout camps will quickly show a boy aiming at a professional career whether or not he has the stuff. There he'll get a far more accurate appraisal of his chances than he will if he continues to play sand-lot ball in the hope that one day he'll catch a talent hunter's eye.

The ambition to be a big-leaguer may be all-consuming, but, as Joe McCarthy said, it takes ambition PLUS skill. The sooner a hopeful youngster finds out he lacks the necessary talent, the better for his whole future. The tryout camp, to my mind, provides one of the best aptitude tests in any field. Immediately the decision is against a candidate, he can begin to equip himself for another career and cease to look upon his current baseball endeavor as only a temporary stopgap until the big-league scout comes along bearing the pot of gold.

This vision of the pot of gold is something that should be examined most clearly by those who seem to have a chance to make the grade. Much publicity has attended the bonuses which have been lavished on the few youngsters who have been paid large sums to sign major-league contracts. Dick Wakefield was a student at the University of Michigan when he received more than $50,000 to sign up with the Detroit Tigers. Several high-school boys have been paid as much as $20,000 to sign a contract. There is talk each year at the winter baseball meetings of the major- and minor-league clubs about outlawing bonuses; but while they have been restricted in many instances, they are still being paid.

If a boy sincerely believes that he has a chance to become a professional ballplayer, he should not haggle too much about a bonus. In saying this I am not fronting for the club owners or trying to conserve their bank balances. As proof, I have held out often enough myself, for I believe that a player's professional life is so short that he is entitled to the high dollar from his club.

But a professional ballplayer holding out in the majors or the minors is in a different position from a young free agent in a tryout camp holding out for a bigger bonus to go into organized ball. The professional fighting for a better contract already is a regular; the youngster is still trying to get his foot in the door. Unless circumstances have placed him in a really strong trading position the youngster shouldn't dull his chances by a bonus battle for a small purse.

The earlier a youngster is launched on a professional career (signed to a contract in organized ball—even in the most lowly rated minor leagues), the earlier he will determine his potentialities and his chances for reaching the majors. And for those who are hopeful of a professional baseball career, there is no future in being a semipro sand lotter or a run-of-the-mill minor-leaguer.

Anyone interested in baseball, be he player or fan, has read about the baseball schools which flourish in various parts of the country. These schools are of two types. One is operated by the baseball clubs themselves, for their own specially selected prospects. The others are privately operated, open to students who pay tuition.

The private schools are operated by active or retired players, such as Rogers Hornsby, who has his classes at Hot Springs, Arkansas, and George Stirnweiss, the Yankees' second baseman, and Joe Stripp, who have their schools in Florida. The tuition is usually about $100, with room and board charged on a non-profit basis.

The instruction at these private schools, as well as at the club schools, is excellent, for the faculties consist of former major-league players who, in most cases, have been operating such classes for several years and not only have acquired the knack of teaching but have developed a training system which is certainly helpful.

Eventual progress of a student into organized baseball depends, of course, upon the individual. But all of these schools are watched by professional scouts, and in most cases the instructors themselves are working officially or unofficially for a club and will tip off their employers at the first sign of talent.

Perhaps the best tribute to the private schools is that many major-league clubs have copied their idea. The Dodgers had a school at the former Pensacola, Florida, naval air base in March, 1947, with an ample faculty of thirty-six to handle the 250 aspiring players who were invited to attend. Among the faculty members was Burt Shotton, who was summoned from the school to manage the Dodgers to their second pennant in twenty-seven years.

The Giants in the spring of 1947 ran a school at Ocala, Florida, for 125 pupils, of whom thirty-seven were good enough to be signed to minor-league contracts. Of these thirty-seven only six failed to finish the season in organized baseball. These results are considered highly satisfactory.

Sometimes there are major-league schools held in the spring to which invitations are unnecessary. The Washington Senators announced such a school for Winter Garden, Florida, from mid-January to mid-February, 1948, with tuition and lodgings free and students required to pay only for their meals, a cost of less than $2 a day. The only limit on enrollment was club approval of written applications.

The fact that major-league clubs go to the expense and effort to conduct schools and tryout camps throughout the year should encourage all who hope for a career in professional baseball. With the farm system growing rapidly and thousands of young players kept out of baseball for several years during the war, there simply is not enough talent to go around. The ball clubs are looking for players—but only if they have the stuff.

No better proof of the intensity of this talent hunt can be offered than the advertisements paid for by the Senators for their Winter Garden school of 1948. It was announced that the school would be directed by Joe Engel, president of the Senators' Chattanooga farm club and head of their scouting system. Engel was advertised as the man who discovered Stanley Harris, Joe Cronin, Ossie Bluege, and Joe Kuhel (all of whom later managed the Senators, with Harris now managing the Yankees and Cronin for years having managed the Red Sox). As a further inducement to apply for enrollment in the school it was stressed that both Cecil Travis and Buddy Lewis came to the

Chattanooga club as amateurs and two years later were major-league stars. Anyone who has played against these two men will testify that the designation "star" is no exaggeration.

Any young ballplayer, whether on a school, sand-lot, or semipro team, who honestly believes that he has a future in professional ball, should place himself under the eyes of major-league observers as soon as possible.

Nor should he allow early disappointments to stand in his way while still in his teens. It is well to remember that many a big-league scout has made a mistake and passed up players who later came to stardom with other major-league clubs. Frank McCormick, who helped Cincinnati win two pennants, was shooed away from tryouts at the Polo Grounds. The Dodgers chased Phil Rizzuto out of Ebbets Field on the grounds that he was too small to be a major-leaguer.

Rizzuto and McCormick, however, were boys when they were turned down. If, by the time he reaches twenty, a player has been told repeatedly that there is no future for him in baseball, it's time for him to accept the decision, take what fun he can from week-end or semipro games, and look elsewhere for a career.

But once he is satisfied that he *can* make the grade, the young player should dedicate himself to preparing for the big chance, always remembering that it means hard work and that for every man such as Bobby Feller who came to the majors a full-fledged star, there are hundreds who must come up the hard way. This means by way of apprenticeship in the minors, often beginning down in Class D, the lowest classification of all.

3: The Minors

IF THE statement "There's plenty of room at the top" is true about most businesses and professions, then baseball is a very singular trade indeed. For baseball has only 400 places at the top—the player limit of the sixteen teams in the two major leagues being at the rate of twenty-five players per team.

For those lucky 400 in the majors the way of living is pleasant. For most of those 7,000 in the minor leagues, however, it's a mean, rough, exhausting grind. For the major-leaguer it's first-class hotels. For the vast majority in the minors it's boardinghouse rooms and doubling up with a teammate. For the majors it's Pullman travel or clean, quick transport planes. For the minors it's a bus or an automobile. For the majors it's the best ball parks and the finest lighting systems in the world. For the minors, too often it's badly kept parks and lights so poor you're lucky if you don't get beaned. For the majors it's a minimum salary of $5,000, and the sky's the limit. For the minors it's as little pay as a thousand dollars for a season.

Old-time vaudeville troupers speak vividly of life on the five-a-day circuit, of the grim rooms in which they slept, their diet of Indian nuts and bread pudding, the laundry they did in bathtubs, their travel in hot, sooty day coaches. But the most unfortunate of those wandering gagsters can't top the old-time minor-leaguers for tales of rugged living.

And with the rarest of exceptions it's the minors which provide the only apprenticeship for a career in professional baseball.

In the rugged living and the discomforts of the minors, baseball is like most other fields of endeavor. The less the performance required, the smaller the return, the meaner the living. The higher the job, the better the pay, the more comfortable the standard of living, the greater the responsibility.

Young players must approach their minor-league apprenticeship with their eyes wide open. It's certainly no picnic to live in the minors, but the player who comes up that way not only has proved himself in professional competition, but has shown that he loves the game deeply enough to accept the toughest sort of existence to reach the top.

From what I have seen in hospitals it's no fun to be an intern either, on call twenty-four hours a day and earning $50 a month. But that's how a young doctor begins to learn the practical side of medicine; and if he doesn't like his profession enough to put up with the discomfort, the inconvenience, and the poverty of his apprenticeship I don't want him practicing on me.

There are six classifications of minor-league baseball, each with different salaries and playing and living conditions. Lowest is Class D, composed of twenty leagues, such as the Alabama State, the Longhorn, the Eastern Shore, the Pony, the Kitty, the Sooner State, and the Tobacco State. The player limit is fifteen, including the manager if he is a player, and the salary limit is $2,250 a month, exclusive of the manager's salary.

Thus the average salary is $150 a month, which is probably less than a job outside baseball, plus a week-end semipro income, would yield. But advancement in baseball proceeds "through channels," just as in the Army or the Navy, as millions of fans and players have had occasion to learn.

The next step up from Class D is Class C, which has fifteen leagues, such as the Arizona-Texas, the Canadian-American, the Pioneer, the Lone Star, the Sunset, and the Cotton States. The player limit it still fifteen, including the manager if he's a player, and the salary limit is $2,800, exclusive of the manager's salary. The extra $550 isn't much when it's spread around among fourteen men, but it's a raise.

Class B, with nine leagues, such as the Three-I, the Inter-State, the Piedmont, the Western International, and the New England, has a player limit of sixteen, including a playing manager, and a salary limit of $3,600, exclusive of the manager's salary.

Class A, which has three leagues, the Eastern, the South Atlantic, and the Western, calls for an eighteen-player roster and a $4,750 top salary; and in Class AA, consisting of the Southern Association and the Texas League, the pay-roll limit is $7,000. As in the lower leagues the manager's salary is outside the pay-roll limit, but he comes under the player quota if he is a playing manager.

It is in the top minor brackets, Double A and Triple A, that a baseball player at last begins to get financial room to breathe. Class AAA is comprised of the American Association, the International Association, and the Pacific Coast League. A top salary for a player in Triple A baseball is approximately $8,500, and in Double A about $6,500, unless he is on option from a major-league club. Then his salary is paid by the big-league club which holds his contract, and the amount is stipulated in that contract.

It is because of the small salaries in the lower minors that a player must make his start in professional baseball while he is still quite young. Only a youngster with little or no family financial responsibility can afford the wages which go with the apprenticeship. The $150-a-month average salary in Class D does not mean $1,800 a year. It is the salary the player receives each month during the playing season.

On such a salary, or a little more, a player must support himself entirely while the club is at home. That means living at a boardinghouse, bunking with a teammate, and watching the nickels and dimes. On the road the team pays for room and meals.

Ballplayers have an extensive and, I feel, unjust reputation as tightwads, although professional baseball has provided as many fabulous spendthrifts as any other field of entertainment. And, as in any other field, the man who has had to count his pennies to make sure there would be a meal tomorrow has certainly learned the amount of sweat that goes into collecting the hundred of them that constitute a dollar; so it is not unreasonable for him to think twice before tossing his dollars around. Moreover, there is a time limit on the earning capacity of a baseball player. Most of them are through as major-leaguers in their thirties. And a lame arm or a broken leg can cut off that earning power overnight. This is not a plea for miserliness, nor is it an apology for reasonable thrift.

Most of my knowledge of life in the lower minors is based on hearsay. I had the good luck to spend my entire minor-league career in the Pacific Coast League, in which all travel and all hotel accommodations are first-class; and with my home-town team, the San Francisco Seals, at that.

Playing on my home-town team meant that when the club played its home stands I could live with my parents, occupy my own room, and eat my meals at the family table. Players not so fortunate as to be playing on their home-town teams must find lodgings where they can, for themselves or for their wives and children. Unless a player is a member of the team representing the city in which he has his permanent residence, he is on the road for the entire baseball season, about seven months of each year.

In most of the lower leagues the jumps from town to town are usually made by bus, sometimes in automobiles and frequently with one of the players doubling as chauffeur. Casey

Stengel, one of the wittiest men in baseball, has some strong advice based on his experiences in his first managerial job, with Providence in the Eastern League, more than twenty years ago. This was the league that Shanty Hogan, the former catcher, called the "Up-and-at-'em" League, "Up all night, at 'em all day." At night, after playing a game under the lights, the team moved on to the next town in automobiles, with four or five players in a car, one of them driving.

"Never let a pitcher who lost a tough game that afternoon be your driver that night," Stengel admonished. "The fellow gets beaten 2 to 1 or 1 to 0. Maybe somebody booted one and cost him the ball game. Maybe the umpire missed a strike on him, or maybe somebody popped up with a chance to win the game. The pitcher gets behind that wheel and he gets brooding over what happened that afternoon. Life doesn't mean anything to him, his or the lives of the guys riding with him. He takes curves at fifty miles an hour and tries to run trucks off the road. What does he care? He just lost a tough ball game."

The one improvement since Stengel's time is that most of the traveling is done by day, since night games are standard fare. In most of the minor leagues there are five night games a week, with a double-header on Sunday. In almost every minor league the players have one regular day off a week, either Monday or Saturday.

Night double-headers are a rough feature of life in the minors. The greater part of the first game will be played in twilight, which for me is the worst possible time to play a game of baseball. As dusk comes there is a sort of false light which makes distances and speeds deceptive, and it is because of this that so many major-league clubs arrange side shows before their night games.

Because almost all of our night games at the Yankee Stadium

in 1946 and 1947 were very nearly if not completely sold out, many fans wondered why Larry MacPhail, the club president, went to the trouble of staging extra attractions such as archery contests before a game. There was simply no more room for any more customers that this extra entertainment might attract.

These stunts were put on deliberately to consume the half hour immediately before game time, which usually is devoted to team practice, because in the tricky light of early evening it was difficult if not impossible to have a workout. Even with the lights on we couldn't judge the speed of a batted or thrown ball, because the lights could not penetrate the false twilight. So in the Yankee Stadium pregame practice was cut down to five minutes for each side after the darkness was sufficiently complete to allow the maximum efficiency of the lighting system.

The lighting systems at the Yankee Stadium and at most major-league parks are superb, and each present system is an improvement over the one used before it. When MacPhail installed lights in Cincinnati in 1935 they were thought to be the last word in artificial illumination for ball games. Since then the installation has been constantly improved.

When I first came to the Yankees in 1936, and we played an occasional exhibition game under lights in a minor-league town, I was still scared to death of getting beaned at the plate even though I had played under lights on the coast. I was always thankful when I finished a night game without getting hurt and grateful that I didn't have to play regularly under such conditions.

The lighting systems of many of the minor-league clubs have improved along with the majors', but there are some places down in Class C or Class D where, I am told, the lights are awful. Under such lights, the scouts say, they can't get any true picture of a game, and one of them told me that he had turned down a pitcher with an amazing strike-out record because this record had been achieved under a lighting system so poor that it made batting difficult, even dangerous.

I don't know if night baseball will ever be popular with players, but since it stimulates attendance so tremendously it is here to stay and probably to expand. It may put the player to personal inconvenience, but since the big receipts from night games go a long way to paying his salary he can't complain too much.

The small pay, the rugged living and traveling conditions, the inferior lighting systems that attend playing in the lower minors aren't intended as a spur to drive the players onward and upward but they certainly must inspire them, in a negative way, to make the most rapid advancement possible. Every player recognizes that the greatest rewards of the professional game are in the major leagues.

It is because of the hardships of the minors that those teams are composed chiefly of players in their teens. Only a youngster, full of the confidence of that age and knowing that if he moves at all it will be upward, can take that sort of living. But even a youngster won't stick around too long in the bushes. There is almost a 100 per cent turnover of personnel on all Class C and Class D teams each year.

There are two main reasons for these sweeping turnovers. One is that if a C or D league player isn't promoted at the season's end, he usually gets out of baseball on his own initiative. The other is that the parent organization, whether a major- or a high minor-league club, sees no percentage in retaining title to a player who doesn't show enough skill to move up one step from the bottom of the ladder after a season's play. The parent club would rather give such a player his unconditional release and make room on the roster for another prospect.

My advice to a boy in C or D ball who doesn't move up at the end of the season is to get out of baseball and look for another career. There may be exceptional cases; for example, an injury, might keep a player out a large part of the season and preclude a true test, but usually if he isn't stepped up a notch it's because he lacks talent.

The parent club is anxious for him to move up as fast as possible, since his value to it is in direct proportion to the caliber of the league in which he is playing. For the player who is "left back" there is no sense in sulking over an imagined injustice. It may be tough for a man to admit that he lacks talent in his chosen field, but it's better than spending the rest of his professional life on benches and busses.

It is the speed with which the young player must develop during his apprenticeship that distinguishes professional baseball from other trades. A playwright may starve for years in the traditional Greenwich Village garret before he writes a Broadway hit, but when he hits, no matter what his age may be, he's at the top. A movie actor may dub around Hollywood in bit parts for season after season, and suddenly get a break and be a candidate for an Oscar. Jim Braddock virtually had retired from the ring and settled down to stevedoring when he came back to defeat Max Baer and win the heavyweight championship of the world.

In moving through the minors, however, the baseball player usually reaches the head of the class quickly or not at all. This does not mean that he should make the majors after a single season in Class D, or even in Triple A, but he should make steady year-to-year progress.

Once above Class C, advancement may be slower, but improvement must continue. The higher the league, the tougher to move through it. To get a good picture of progress through professional baseball, regard the entire minor-league system as a huge funnel, with the Class D clubs at the open end and the Triple A at the tube, through which a few players trickle to the majors each year. Players in the funnel must concentrate on getting closer and closer to the tube.

In Class B and higher leagues a player may show definite improvement and still not advance to a better classification. But after a couple of seasons in Class B he should be ready to move along or make a determined effort to learn the reason why.

The laws of baseball are written to ensure his advancement if he has the ability. There is, for instance, the draft. If he has played for three years in the minors, or if he has been in the majors and has been returned to the minors, he is eligible to be drafted by another major-league team for the draft price, which varies for the different minor leagues.

The whole purpose of the draft law is to prevent a club from "covering up" its minor-league players who have shown definite big-league ability. For example, a player is a top-notch first baseman in Triple A, but the major-league team which holds his contract has a first baseman with whom it is well satisfied.

Were it not for the draft the Triple A star might languish there throughout his career, or until the first baseman on the parent club finished his playing days. Under the draft rules, however, the parent club must bring the Triple A man up and give him a chance to win the job or sell him to another major-league team. Failing to do this, the owning club runs the risk of losing him in the draft for $10,000—which in these days is chicken feed for the contract of a standout player in Triple A.

The draft not only safeguards a player against being stalled in the minors if he has the skill to move up, but it also provides for him the best possible chance to judge for himself whether he has that skill or not.

Almost everyone who plays any athletic game, as a profession or for amusement, considers himself a little better performer than he really is; he rates himself on the basis of his peak performance, achieved only on better days. Just go to the nearest golf club and you will find players who regularly score above 100 describing themselves as 95-players because once in a blue moon they get down to 95.

Minor-leaguers, like other athletes, have the same exaggerated regard for their abilities, but the draft hands down a judgment that cannot be contradicted. If the player is not brought up by the parent club there may be a reason for it, such as plenty of strength in his particular position, but when he is subject to the draft every other club will be angling for him if he has the stuff. If he is repeatedly passed over in the draft it means that several competent, player-hungry judges have decided against him, and he will be smart if he decides that baseball is not his profession, although it may be his sport.

There are, however, a few players who make a comfortable living in the upper-bracket minors each summer. Leagues in Class A and up are out of the bus circuit, the ball parks are better, the hotels in which the teams are housed are good, and there is always a chance of a career as a manager. Several minor-league teams have managers under thirty.

The player with real managerial ability has tremendous prospects, even though he may lack the physical skill to accomplish big-league plays. Joe McCarthy, who has won more pennants and World Series than any other manager, never played ball in the majors.

Even in the minors he was not a top-flight ballplayer, by his own admission, but he supplemented his limited playing skill with shrewd observations, and his natural intelligence made it plain that his baseball future was in managing rather than in playing. As a manager he won pennants in all minor-league classifications, and at Louisville, in the American Association, he did such an outstanding job that he was brought up to the Chicago Cubs.

McCarthy has rare talent as a handler of players and as director of a team, and, while there are few McCarthys, his success indicates the possibilities of a career in baseball other than as a player. The man who cannot hope to make the major-league grade on the basis of playing skill may find another job in baseball if he studies all angles of the game seriously and closely observes the operations of his own and opposing managers.

Many major-league coaches and scouts have had little playing experience in the majors but bring fine minor-league training to their jobs. This is a field to which the player of limited skill might very well turn his attention, for with the growth of the farm system and with the constantly increasing talent hunt, the chances for such employment have increased.

The average ballplayer, in the majors or the minors, is suspicious of the farm system because it seems to put so many of them under the control of one major-league club. The farm, however, is a part of baseball that is here to stay. It is the world's greatest source of potential big-league players.

With the exception of the Pacific Coast League, all of the Triple A clubs and most of the clubs in lower leagues are owned outright by major-league clubs or have working agreements with them.

There are individual cases in which a player suffers some injustice because his club is owned by a farm system, but such cases are few, and the player always has the draft law working in his corner if he is detained too long in the minors. The biggest handicap of the farm system in so far as the individual player is concerned is that it increases the competition for the major-league berth on which he has set his eye. When he finally gets to the parent club's spring training camp he is likely to find a number of other candidates for the same job, and from leagues in classifications as high as his own.

There is no major-league club today that doesn't have connections with a dozen minor-league teams, and usually the figure is closer to two dozen. Parent teams lucky enough to find themselves overstocked with minor-league talent in specific positions peddle off their excess players to other clubs. The existence of the draft law, which guards against the covering up of players, prevents the farm system from being a dangerous monopoly which could keep a player down in the minors throughout his career.

The farm system has certainly brought to the minors a higher brand of instruction. Minor-league managers know they are expected to develop major-league players, and unless they show ability to work with and improve young ballplayers they don't keep their jobs too long.

Unless a man is a pitcher or a catcher he has little chance to graduate from the minors without speed of foot and a good throwing arm. He can reasonably expect to improve his skills at hitting, fielding, and base running, provided he is endowed with these two natural attributes.

In the majors and in the minors pitchers are in a class all by themselves. A pitcher who can throw hard always has a chance to become a major-leaguer no matter how often he is turned back. The principal reason that he makes good with one big-league team after several others have rejected him is that at last he has acquired control. Few pitchers are born with it, and none is any good until he masters it. There are always pitchers in the minors who have enough *stuff* to win in the majors except for the horrible fact that they can't get the ball over the plate. Some of them eventually acquire control and go on to become big-league winners. Others never get it.

There are also in the minors, even in the upper-bracket leagues, pitchers who are consistent winners but who never get a tumble from the majors. Usually they are the unlucky ones who did not acquire their control until the hop had left their fast ball and the snap had gone from their curve. What they have left of their stuff, plus their control, is enough to win for them in the minors, but not in the majors.

Thus a pitcher with stuff always has a chance to reach the majors, provided that he gets control. Dazzy Vance lingered in the minors for years, suddenly found himself, went up to the Dodgers and led the National League in strike-outs for several seasons. Carl Hubbell was turned back twice by the Detroit Tigers before the Giants took him on.

Pitchers are the only ones, however, who can take so much time to make the grade. Players at other positions, unless they're brought up after four or five years in the minors, have little chance. Once in a great while an infielder or an outfielder more than thirty years old is brought up to the majors, but it is usually for a spot emergency, and he rarely stays up very long. The Dodgers once brought up an infielder who had spent thirteen seasons in the minors, but he didn't make a good infielder. On the other hand, there are many pitchers who have come through after thirty. Notable among them are Cy Moore of the Yankees of Miller Huggins's day and Jim Turner and Lou Fette of the Braves of 1936.

An infielder, an outfielder, or a catcher can help himself along in the minors by careful comparison of his own performance with those of the other players at his position in his league. If there is a standout in that position his play should be observed closely to learn how he makes the play, and his speed and other physical attributes should be tallied. A smart player is always a learner. He should seek guidance and correction of faults from teammates and manager, and not stand around and wait to be corrected.

As soon as he gets into the lower minors a player should set rigid standards for his performance. In Class C and Class B he hasn't much hope for advancement unless he is among the top two or three in the league at his position. In Class A and up he must be far above the average to advance.

Baseball can yield big dividends at the top; a terrible grind is the only pay-off for mediocrity.

4: The Majors

In the majors there are no soft spots, no glaring weaknesses among the players, no individual players whose known faults can be counted on to give an opponent a breathing spell. The brand of competition is far hotter than in the minors—hotter, I believe, than in any other level of team athletics in the world. Every batter is a threat to ram the ball out of the park, every pitcher a potential wrecker of a team's winning streak.

That is the best answer to the question the minor-leaguer invariably asks the major-leaguer: "What's the difference up there?"

One of the soundest descriptions of this difference that I have ever found came from a pitcher who had gone to a major-league training camp in 1933, my first year with the San Francisco Seals. When he reached the majors, one of the California papers interviewed him, and his observations impressed me so much that I still remember the gist of them:

"In the minors I could pitch to spots fairly often. There were batters who couldn't do anything with a low pitch, others who couldn't do anything with one inside, and so on. Up here I don't think there are any hitters with a pronounced over-all batting weakness. If they were complete dubs at the plate they wouldn't be in the big leagues even with sensational fielding skill that sometimes carries weak hitters. On the other hand every batter has one certain alley in which he can overpower the ball better than in another. I intend to pitch away from that spot, away from his strength."

This man was the smartest pitcher I had ever watched before I came to the majors, but despite his excellent operating plan he couldn't make the big-league grade as a regular. He lacked the physical equipment to prove his theory in the major leagues.

Although I did all my minor-league playing with the Seals, in Triple A, the highest minor classification, the difference in competition which I encountered with the Yankees was immediately obvious.

The absence of glaring weaknesses among the batters, most pitchers excepted, is indeed the big distinction. The absence of soft spots is true of second-division as well as first-division clubs, and even of tailenders. The major-league player cannot let down.

Every fan knows how often a .220 hitter breaks up a ball game with a line drive out of sight, or how frequently a pitcher with an ordinary record strikes out a star batter in a tight spot.

With the Seals, whenever we opened a series, I could count on a couple of pitchers on the opposing team, rarely more than two, who could make it tough for me. Once I got by those two I didn't have much to worry about. In the major leagues every opposing pitcher has a good chance to wrap you up in horse collars.

It is thus also with the hitters. A minor-league pitcher usually faces a few spots in the opposing batting order in which he knows that he can relax. In the majors a pitcher doesn't dare get careless with the man batting seventh or eighth, regardless of how puny that hitter's average might be.

Once I asked Red Ruffing, a top-flight competitor, why he frequently bore down so hard on the tail end of the batting order.

"Those are the guys," he said, "who break your heart when they get a hit off of you, because you figure they're not entitled to it. So I made up my mind long ago that if any of the weak ones were going to get a hit off of me they were going to have to hit my Sunday stuff." However, most pitchers do not have Ruffing's strength and find it necessary to let up occasionally on the tailenders.

The rookie coming up to the major leagues will have something else to contend with besides the smart pitches and the big bats. It's something that he can't see, or beat with a bat, or catch in his glove, but it's there—a lump in his throat, a butterfly in his stomach, a shake in his knees, a pool of sweat in his hands. It's pressure, and the more the publicity which has accompanied him to the majors the more the pressure.

The man isn't human who doesn't feel it. Because I had been signed by the Yankees two years before I came to their training camp at St. Petersburg in 1936, I had received a tremendous ballyhoo. Although I was being called "Dead Pan" I know I sweated it out as much as the most jittery, rubber-faced boy in camp. I had been glad enough to get all the notice during my last two years in the minors, but when I reached St. Petersburg I actually envied other rookies who had come into camp without the big blast.

Every rookie who has been bought for a large sum or who brings up an imposing minor-league record will feel the pressure more than the one who virtually sneaks into camp. It's especially true if the publicity throughout the preceding winter has "assured" him of a starting position.

A prime example of the result of pressure was found in the opening-day game between the Dodgers and the Boston Braves in 1947. Earl Torgeson, the Braves' first baseman, had been bought by Boston two years earlier. The Dodgers started Spider Jorgensen at third base. He had been on the roster of their Montreal farm club until the day before.

Torgeson was conscious of all that was expected of him. He struck out twice and had an off day in the field. Jorgensen played a great game and got a couple of extra-base hits. He broke into the major-league line-up so quickly that the pressure had no chance to pile up on him. As it usually does, it wore off quickly with Torgeson, and he proved to be a real first baseman for the Braves.

There is nothing that a rookie can do to escape the nervous pressure that comes with unaccustomed circumstances of play. It's on him the first day he gets to camp, no matter how kindly he may be treated by his new manager, his new teammates, and the reporters covering the club. He shakes it off as he makes good during the training season, and it returns all over again when he starts his first game.

Everyone will advise him to relax, which is tough advice to put into operation. I believe the pressure on him disappears when he has made his first play successfully. When a batter gets hold of one, when a fielder drags in a fly, when a pitcher gets the ball where he wants it, he stops shaking and begins to enjoy playing ball again.

The first thing to which a rookie should turn his attention when he reports to a training camp is getting in shape. Running and working out at every opportunity will help to take the pressure away, for when he gets to bed at night he'll be so tired physically that he'll be asleep before he has a chance to toss and turn and worry over making the grade.

Players who have reached the rung in the ladder represented by a big-league camp may think they know all the dangers of rushing into action too soon, but trainers in every camp nurse dozens of sore arms for rookies too anxious to make an impression before they are really ready to cut loose.

Although the routine of spring training is calculated to eliminate the danger, there has never yet been a training camp without its quota of sore arms and Charley horses. Charley horses, those painful and annoying muscle pulls, are only temporary afflictions, but that doesn't mean that precautions shouldn't be taken against them, too. Any time a rookie is forced to the side lines of a training camp, even if only for a few days, he is losing valuable time while his competitors are making progress.

The first impression a rookie gets of spring training is the monotonous routine of conditioning. He runs and runs, shags flies until he is ready to drop, then gets a brief turn at batting practice, hitting a few balls served up by a pitcher who isn't trying to put anything on it but is just getting it across the plate. Pitchers warm up constantly. Warnings against cutting loose are called out all over the place.

The manager, of course, is trying to bring the entire squad into shape at the same time. A few privileged veterans may be allowed to take things easy; the boss has confidence in their experience and ability to get themselves into condition in their own way.

In the early games the teams will be made up principally of pitchers, with a few catchers or outfielders playing the infield. To balance the competition, if one team is made up largely of rookies a veteran will do the pitching; if the other team consists chiefly of regulars, a rookie will be its pitcher.

More frequently, however, rookies will pitch for all teams, since rookie pitchers form the largest single group in a training camp, and the manager wants to see the work of as many of them as possible. They can pitch only at intervals, and he can inspect the performances of his infield, outfield, and catching candidates every day.

When the exhibition games start, the hard-working rookie will find that he has brought himself into shape without realizing that he has reached playing condition.

The exhibition games also will bring a stepped-up tempo of competition. In the first exhibition games, perhaps the first ten, rookies or the previous year's second-stringers will probably handle the pitching. The work of the previous season's regulars already is known to the manager.

The pitchers in the early exhibition games usually are ahead of the hitters, farther advanced in conditioning because they had a head start of a week or so in training. Rookie batters will find them tough to hit against. So will the regulars.

The real test comes when the hitters begin to catch up with the pitchers. This is also the time that gives meaning to the ancient baseball gag about the rookie who wired his mother: "Will be home soon, Mom. They're starting to curve me."

The rookie of today is relieved of the hazing that was once the unhappy lot of every busher who came to a major-league club. The principal reason for the elimination of hazing as a part of the routine of the game is that the clubs today want to develop their young players to maximum efficiency with maximum haste and tolerate nothing that hinders them.

Under Joe McCarthy and Bucky Harris, the managers for whom I've played in the majors, there would be no putting up with the stunt of which Babe Ruth himself was the victim when he first joined the Red Sox. Some of the veterans thought he was taking too much time at the plate in batting practice, and one day he went to his locker to find all his bats sawed neatly in quarters.

It's as difficult to imagine that happening today as it is to think of the college-boy or ex-G.I. rookies we get now falling for the worn-out snipe-hunt gag. The only hazing that goes on now, if it can be called that, is on a par with leaving a fake telephone number for a rookie, who calls it to find that he has reached the mayor or the local cemetery.

When a rookie reaches a major-league camp he finds a manager who knows as much about him as he knows about himself. The manager has received a full report on him from two or three scouts. If he comes from the club's farm the manager has complete reports on him from the time he entered the system, or even from his first tryout.

This is helpful to the newcomer, especially if he gets off to a poor start. It's not as if he were a complete unknown trying to impress the manager. From the thorough reports the manager can tell if the rookie is playing below his minor-league form, pressing, perhaps, in his desire to make good.

Moreover, the scout on whose recommendation the rookie has been brought up probably is on hand. And since this scout is largely responsible for the youngster's presence there, he will take a personal interest in advising him and helping him to make him feel at home.

One of the most important achievements of a young baseball career is to impress the manager well the first time up. If the rookie does that it is not too damaging to him if he doesn't stick on his initial try; he may be sure that he will be called back the next year, when he has had the benefit of another season of experience, and when the regular he is being groomed to succeed has slowed up by just that much.

I know of no statistics on the odds against a rookie's making the team the first time he comes to a major-league training camp. To figure these odds, even approximately, I have eliminated those who try out but never succeed. Of the ones who do make good I believe that about three-fourths of them had more than one try, that only a fourth of them made it their first time up.

Of those who are given a second chance, it seems to me just from looking around that about half of them make good. But after the second trial the chances of making it are very slight, judged by the number of players who have done it. After the second trial the law of diminishing returns sets in.

Rookies who fail to stick their first time up can find plenty of comfort in the records of some of their greatest predecessors.

The great Babe Ruth, sent to the Red Sox from Baltimore in midsummer of 1914, stayed a month and was optioned to Providence. Ted Williams, one of the finest natural hitters in the history of the game, was sent back to the minors for a season after his first trip to a Red Sox training camp. Both Pittsburgh and Cincinnati returned shortstop Eddie Miller to the minors before he finally made good with the Braves. Al Lopez, who broke all endurance records for catchers, was sent down twice by the Dodgers before he established himself in the National League. The Yankees returned George McQuinn to Newark, chiefly because they had Lou Gehrig at first base, and Cincinnati sent him down again before he came back to star with the St. Louis Browns when they won their only pennant, in 1944. And he had been made a free agent by the Philadelphia Athletics when he was taken on by the Yankees and played a big part in winning the pennant in 1947.

This list can be extended to include hundreds of others over the years. A mathematically-minded researcher probably can come up with a much more exact figure of the odds against a rookie's making good than my guesswork formula of four to one the first time and even money the second, but it will be better for a candidate's confidence if he looks at it this way: few rookies make good in their first shot at a big-league job. About half of those who go to a major-league training camp can reasonably expect to get a second chance if they fail on the first trial. A player may be released by a major-league club, or even two, and still become a big-league regular, but the chances are heavily against it.

The option rule plays a big part in the manner in which a major-league club disposes of its rookies. After a player has been in the minors for three years he must be recalled by the parent club and may not be sent down again except on option.

This means that the major-league club holds his contract and pays his salary, which is at least $5,000, the major-league minimum. He may not be optioned more than three times. After that he must be sold to another major-league club, made a free agent or released outright to a minor-league club, and any major-league team can bid for him.

No major-league team may have more than eight players on option at one time. Every player brought to a major-league training camp must be signed to a major-league contract. Since most major-league teams bring a minimum of a dozen rookies to their camps in the spring, that means that at least four must be retained or sold outright.

The case of Jackie Robinson, the first Negro player signed to a contract in organized baseball in modern times, is an excellent example of the workings of baseball law. The Brooklyn Dodgers signed him to a contract with their Montreal farm club. He had a terrific season with Montreal in 1946, leading the International League in hitting, leading the second basemen in fielding, and stealing more than forty bases. Yet he was not among the Montreal players recalled by the Dodgers at the end of the 1946 season.

The reason was that it was technically advantageous to the Dodgers not to recall him. Since 1946 was his first year in organized baseball, he was not subject to the draft. If he had been recalled and failed to make good at the 1947 training camp he could have been sent back only on option or as the property of the Montreal club, and as minor-league property, up once in the majors, he would have been eligible to be picked up in the draft for only $10,000, the standard draft price for Triple A players. Ten thousand dollars for Jackie Robinson! Moreover, since a major-league club may have only forty players under contract between September 15 and May 1, the Dodgers had room for one more man on their roster by not recalling him.

Robinson went to spring training in 1947 with Montreal. When his work there made it clear that he had the stuff to help the Dodgers, they bought him from Montreal a few days before the 1947 season opened. The purchasing of his contract from a club which the Dodgers own is just another example of the complex business side of baseball.

When a rookie finally has made the grade, when he has fought his way through the narrow tube of the funnel into the top playing ranks of organized baseball, he will find that life in the majors is just what the term "big league" implies.

He will sleep in top hotels, travel comfortably, eat well. (And he'll have the money to eat heartily even when the club is not picking up the check on the road.) His daily work will be sports-page news throughout the country. Baseball is a team game, first, last, and always, but recognition of an individual contribution to the team's success is surely gratifying. The deliberate headline hunter will soon find he is pretty lonesome, but the performer who doesn't really get a bang out of a compliment is an unusual human being.

Travel by air has increased tremendously in the major leagues since the war. Starting in the middle of the 1946 season the Yankees used planes for a whole year, including cross-Caribbean flights for spring-training dates in Panama, Puerto Rico, Venezuela, and Cuba. The Red Sox flew most of their team from Boston to St. Louis for the sixth and seventh games of the 1946 World Series. The Dodgers flew to their 1946 and 1947 training bases.

I like flying because I get where I'm going in a hurry, but a lot of players have sincere objections to it. Some of them just don't like getting up in a plane. Others object to stalling around an airport, waiting for clearance. Many gripe at the meals, which satisfy most people. The average ballplayer likes a lot of everything. Airplane space does not provide for storing and cooking forty steaks, each the size of a first baseman's mitt.

Players coming up from the minors will find more and more that one phase of baseball in the majors is familiar to them. That's night ball. The Yankees in 1947 scheduled only twenty-eight night games, two at home and two on the road, with each club in the league. The financial necessities of other cities, however, force heavier night schedules. Night games definitely make baseball available to a larger number of fans. Men who would have to neglect their business to go to a weekday afternoon game now come out at night. They bring their wives, which makes for more and more fans among women. Although night ball may upset a player's living schedule, it certainly stimulates attendance, and the player has to benefit by the increased gate.

I believe most players feel as I do: that they would rather have only afternoon games or only night games, not a lot of each. The minor-league schedule of five night games and one daylight double-header a week may be the solution. Arranging eating and sleeping schedules during a mixture of both night and day games such as the Yankees ran into for one stretch in our nineteen-game winning streak in 1947 would give a certified public accountant a headache.

In St. Louis, we played a night game on Thursday, a twilight game on Friday, and a double-header Saturday afternoon. We took a sleeper to Chicago, played a double-header Sunday afternoon and a night game Monday, then took a midnight train to Cleveland. That meant we went to bed at 2 A.M. one day, midnight or later the next four days, and had dinner at 3 P.M., 9 P.M., 7 P.M., 8 P.M., and 3 P.M.

There is an old baseball story about Tim Hurst, who was asked why he decided on a career as a baseball umpire.

"You can't beat the hours, three to five," he replied.

The hours have changed since Tim Hurst's day, but you can't beat the game itself.

5: First Base

THE GENERAL prescription for a first baseman would be that he is "long, lean, and left-handed," but the prescription is only occasionally followed. It's like the old story of the rookie ballplayer who made his first sleeper jump on a Pullman. He asked the porter what was the average tip and was told that it was a dollar. He gave the porter a dollar and the porter said, "Thank you, sir. And I might say you're the first who has come up to the average in some time."

So it is with first basemen. Not all of them are long, some are not lean, and many are not left-handed.

The advantage of a left-handed-throwing first baseman is obvious. Almost all of a first baseman's throwing plays are to his right side, which means that he doesn't have to turn awkwardly to make the throw if he is a left-hander.

The throws to second and third on bunts and force plays, particularly on sacrifice bunts, are invariably split-second affairs, and the advantage of not having to turn frequently determines the difference between a runner's being safe or out.

For a left-handed first baseman the most difficult play is fielding a ball thrown to his left, up the first-base line and into the runner. It is on this play alone that the right-handed first baseman has an advantage. All the right-hander has to do is to anchor his right foot on the base and stretch in the direction of home plate. The glove, being on his left hand, is in a natural position to take the throw, and all he has to do is to bring his right foot forward and pivot with the runner.

A throw "into the runner" does not mean that the ball hits

the runner but that it is thrown in the path in which he is running and at the objective toward which he is heading.

Consider now the position of a left-hander on the same play. He usually has his left foot on the bag, his right foot extended as far as possible toward the player who makes the throw. He then stretches as far as he can with his gloved (right) hand to

FIRST BASEMAN'S NIGHTMARE: STRETCHING OVER THE FOUL LINE INTO THE RUNNER FOR A THROW FAR TO HIS LEFT. HE TWISTS HIS NECK TO FOLLOW THE BALL OVER RIGHT SHOULDER AND MAKES A BACK-HAND CATCH

take the ball. The farther to his left he must stretch, the more he must turn his back to the thrower, until he is virtually watching the ball over his right shoulder. It requires greater agility for a man in this position to untangle himself and get off the bag in time to avoid bumping the runner than it does for the right-handed fielder.

From time to time there have been some good right-handed-throwing first basemen in the major leagues, and it has always been on this play that they have shown to the best advantage. Since the throw to second or third is so important, however, the left-hander is preferred. The first baseman is called on to make a throw across the diamond far more often than he has to take a throw up the line and into the base runner.

In stressing throws to the first baseman's left and into the runner, I'm talking about plays which are close—"bang-bang" plays, we call them, meaning that the ball bangs into the glove and the runner's foot bangs into the bag almost simultaneously. Almost simultaneously, because in baseball, as an old umpire once put it, "There are no ties—either you're safe or you ain't."

On throws into the runner when the play isn't close, the first baseman can take the throw off the bag and then step back, tagging the bag, and his worries are over. It goes without saying that only close plays are difficult—all the others are routine.

The great value of a top-notch first baseman, whether right-handed or left-handed, lies in his ability to stretch and make pickups, i.e., fielding the throw on the short hop immediately after it has struck the ground. The pickups made by a first baseman differ entirely from those made by any other infielder, or any outfielder, for that matter, because the first baseman makes his pickups while his body is stationary, his foot anchored on the bag. Other fielders may be in motion as they make a pickup, charging the ball or backing up from it.

There is no rule in baseball older than "Keep your eye on the ball." In the pickup by a first baseman, it is of highest importance. He must have flexible wrists, skillful hands, and a sure sense of touch and timing. He must close in on the ball, with both hands if possible, the instant it leaves the ground. In many cases, he must make the pickup with his glove hand alone.

Some first basemen toss off the gloved-hand pickup as a "you-do-or-you-don't" play; that is, its successful accomplishment is no more than a lucky stab. Since top-notch first basemen "do," however, more often than they "don't," the success of this play indicates skill rather than luck.

The importance of the stretch is obvious. Since so many plays at first base are decided by an eyelash, the first baseman with the longer stretch is getting his hands on the ball more quickly than the first baseman who breaks his elbows and takes the ball in close to his body. There is no prettier sight in baseball than a first baseman, fully extended, doing an acrobatic split that would do credit to a ballet dancer, and coming up with the ball on the short hop just a half step ahead of a runner. No prettier sight, that is, for all except the team at bat.

More than any other player on the team, a first baseman is required to be shifty on his feet. He must shift his feet with every thrown ball so as to get the maximum stretch to receive the throw. Picture a play on which he can take the ball with both hands—that is, when it is directly in front of him or on his glove side. He dashes to the bag as soon as the ball is hit to another infielder and places both heels against the corner of the bag facing the direction from which the throw is expected. When the throw comes to the left side of the bag, the first baseman keeps his right foot on the bag, stretches forward as far as possible with his left and takes the throw. The procedure, of course, is reversed when the throw comes from the right side.

On throws which he has to take with his gloved hand alone, far to his left if he is left-handed, to his right if he is right-handed, he must twist his body until his back is to the thrower, peer over his shoulder to follow the ball and take it backhanded in his glove. This is exactly the procedure mentioned before, which a left-handed-fielding first baseman must follow on throws into the runner. Here it applies to either right-handed or left-handed fielders.

Shifting is a real art, demanding the nimbleness and agility, in its own way, of an intricate dance step. It can be mastered only by constant practice. Constant practice, of course, is necessary for the development of any special talent, but the shift and the stretch are requirements peculiar to the first-base position, and no first baseman can afford to overlook any opportunity to improve himself along these lines.

Some of the most agile players in baseball history have been first basemen—George Sisler, Bill Terry, Joe Kuhel, Dolph Camilli, Harry Davis, Joe Judge, Babe Dahlgren, and Hal Chase, to name a few. Of those mentioned, Dahlgren is the only right-hander, which shows how the average runs. Babe, incidentally, had as good a glove hand as any first baseman. He used to make some remarkable left-handed stabs, the glove, of course, being on his left hand.

The reason a first baseman should be nimble and agile is simple. He has to take more bad throws, and in more awkward positions, than anybody else on the team. If he's born graceful, it's a big help.

On the subject of awkward positions and bad throws, and in relation to the stretch, the low throw which strikes the ground so far in front of the first baseman that it can't be fielded on a pickup needs special mention. If the first baseman is stretched out for such a throw it will bound over his head and get beyond him completely. This is a play which the first baseman sometimes has to field in foul territory, keeping one foot on the base and stepping backward with the other to take the throw on a bigger hop.

Judgment is essential in such a play, of course, as judgment is essential in other plays relating to bad throws. A first baseman must know precisely, not approximately, how far he can stretch for a throw. There are times when it will be necessary to come off the bag and take a throw to keep it from getting by him and going to the stands. Remember that it is sounder by far to come off the bag and take a bad throw, allowing the hitter to reach first, than it is to let the throw get by with the hitter going all the way to third, to say nothing of the runners already on base being able to score.

The question of how far a first baseman should play off the bag when there is no runner on first depends upon the ability of the first baseman, the speed with which he can return to the bag, and the composition of his infield.

It may seem at first glance that the question of playing off the bag can be settled entirely by the first baseman himself, but this isn't always so. Some infielders have a habit of firing the ball as soon as they get their hands upon it, and provision must be made for them. Pie Traynor was one of these. Charley Grimm, a real first baseman, tells this story of the first time he played in the same infield with Traynor, at Pittsburgh:

"We were playing the Giants at the Polo Grounds in 1921, and on the first ball hit to Traynor he scooped it up and flung it to first almost in one motion, so that I had to catch the ball in self-defense or be skulled with it. Furthermore, it seemed to me that Pie had scooped up everything in the Polo Grounds—grass, dust, and gravel—and flung it over to first with the ball. It was like a sandstorm."

Traynor went on to be one of the greatest third basemen of all time, but he never got over the habit of throwing the ball as soon as he fielded it. He could never take advantage of any time he had on a play to steady himself and line up a throw. He said that if he took his time with a throw, even on an easy play, he invariably threw the ball wildly.

On the subject of playing off the bag, the safest rule for a first baseman to follow is never to play so far from the bag that he has trouble getting back in time for the quickest throw. The "in time" angle is important, because on most infield plays the first baseman should be on the bag in time to give the infielder a target. It is far easier for the infielder to locate a 6-foot, 200-

pound man than to spot a 1-foot-square white canvas bag.

Lou Gehrig had quite a lot of difficulty in gauging his distance from the bag when he first came up with the Yankees. Lou, eager and conscientious, wanted to cover the last possible inch of territory, and he had a tendency to roam too far to his right to plug the hole between first and second. He ran into two difficulties: he sometimes couldn't get back to the base in time to take the throw if another man fielded the ball, and if he did field it himself he would often be out of position to throw it back in time to nail the runner. Either way, an infield hit that could have been converted into a put-out became a safety.

Gehrig was a persevering ballplayer. He practiced and practiced until he taught himself exactly how far he could go off the bag. Finally he fixed in his mind a point off the bag from which he could go two strides for balls batted to his right. If the ball was hit farther than two strides to his right, Lou would dig for the bag immediately and allow the second baseman to handle the ball.

The distance a first baseman can play off the bag depends to a great extent on the fielding ability and cooperation of the pitcher. And since pitchers vary more widely in fielding ability than players in any other position, the first baseman must adjust his distance from the bag to the fielding ability of every pitcher who happens to be working.

If the pitcher is agile and can break off the rubber on balls hit between the mound and first base, the first baseman can allow himself more latitude in going to his right. If the pitcher is slow coming off the rubber, the first baseman can't go too far to his right, because if he does there will be no one covering first base, even though he fields the ball.

Playing off the bag brings up another delicate problem peculiar to first base: that of feeding the ball to the pitcher after the first baseman has made the stop and the pitcher has gone to the bag to take the throw. Many a put-out is lost at first base because the pitcher, even though he takes the throw, fails to touch the bag in crossing it.

Pitchers, as a class, are notoriously clumsy fielders, although some have functioned so well as to be called "fifth infielders." If possible, get the ball to the pitcher so he can take it a couple of steps before he reaches the bag. Having made the catch, he then can concentrate on locating the bag. Timing is as essential here as it is for a football forward passer in leading his receiver.

Some pitchers prefer a lob throw, others want the ball thrown hard, or at least with a reasonable amount of speed. It is a matter of the individual pitcher's likes and dislikes, and one more problem for the first baseman—he must remember the type of throw each pitcher prefers on this play.

When a first baseman has fielded a ball so far from the bag that he can't get back in time, and the pitcher must cover the base, he should wheel into throwing position instantly, getting the ball away as fast as is feasible. The sooner the pitcher gets the ball, the less trouble his feet are going to have finding the bag.

One of the prettiest plays in baseball, and therefore one which is most difficult to execute perfectly, is the double play from first to second to first. Fans often hear it called the "3-6-3" play by baseball writers and broadcasters because that is the way it is scored, "3" being the scoring symbol for the first baseman and "6" for the shortstop. Although the double play is from first to second to first, it is the shortstop who handles the ball at second base.

On this play, the first baseman must field the ball, throw it quickly to the shortstop, usually having the additional difficulty of throwing around the base runner, and then get back to first in time to take the return throw. The play is almost impossible to make unless the ball is hit hard and is fielded clean by the first baseman. On rare occasions, an adroit pitcher may get off the mound in time to take the relay from the short-stop, but no first baseman can afford to count on this.

One of the real masters of this play was Bill Terry of the Giants, and he said that the play gave him so much trouble when he first broke into baseball that he seriously considered quitting first base and going back to being a pitcher. The phase of the play which gave Terry so much difficulty in his younger days was the throw to second. Terry always was a sure fielder with his glove and had unusual speed. Fielding the ball and get-ting back to first base were no problems, but getting the ball to the shortstop was.

Terry practiced the play over and over in his minor-league days. While playing for Toledo he persuaded a coach and a couple of teammates to come for practice in the morning so he could work on the play. The coach acted as the runner on first base. The very first practice session ended when one of Terry's throws conked the coach behind the ear and knocked him un-conscious. It was a long time before Terry could get anybody to work with him again, but he finally became one of the best in the business at the play. Joe Judge of the Senators was a past master at the first-to-second-to-first double play, one of the greatest ever to execute it.

The big trick in this first-second-first double play, of course, is getting back to first base for the shortstop's throw. The field-ing of the batted ball and the throw to second should eventually become routine, but once the first baseman has made the throw he must break quickly for the bag. And the return throw must be taken with a minimum of time and with little opportunity for the first baseman to set himself, as in the case of ordinary plays at first base.

Getting back to the base under these conditions means that the first baseman must know where the bag is, since he must line it up in one quick glance. He's not just running, he's running for the bag. This judgment of distance also is essential on foul flies hit to the first baseman's territory, particularly short pop-ups which the first baseman must hustle to get under. Good first basemen recommend taking one quick glance at the stands to gauge how far they can run, then going after the ball. On the home field, a first baseman has a fairly accurate idea of how far he can go in pursuit of a foul, but on the road it is a good idea to take that one flash peek at the stands.

In the matter of gloves, it is up to the player himself to provide himself with a mitt which he can handle comfortably and deftly. Hank Greenberg played first base for Detroit with a glove so large that rival managers called it the "crab net," and there even was some talk of protesting to the league that it was illegal. Yet when Greenberg went to the outfield for the Tigers, and Rudy York played first, York wore a glove that looked hardly larger than the mitten used by the motorman of a trolley car.

Position play is all important for a first baseman, and the circumstances of the game govern the position. With a runner on first, or runners on first and second, the position of the first baseman changes radically. His first duty, of course, is to hold the runner on base.

The conditions of the game at the time—the score, the number of outs, the inning—usually determine whether the next hitter will attempt a sacrifice bunt. There are few surprise bunts with a man on first. Unless there is none out, it is one hundred to one against the bunt. Sometimes, but not very often, with one out and a man on first, a bunt may be attempted if the pitcher is the batter. The theory behind this is that the pitcher is a weak hitter and a slow runner and that if he did hit the ball to the infield, it would be an almost certain double play. Under those conditions, a manager sometimes will have the pitcher bunt, gambling on the next batter to score the runner from second with a single.

If there is none out with a runner on first, the first baseman usually plays with his right foot on a corner of the bag, his left foot in foul territory. He crouches, so as to break for the plate on the anticipated bunt. The first few steps of the first baseman's charge should be enough for him to determine whether the batter is going to bunt. If the batter assumes a bunting position, the first baseman continues his dash to the plate; otherwise he stops in his tracks.

With a runner on first and no bunt anticipated, the first baseman holds the runner on in the normal position but, as the ball is pitched, he breaks toward second, instead of charging the plate. If the batter is a dead-right-field pull-hitter, the first baseman may hold the runner on by playing directly behind the bag and then backpedaling as the ball is delivered.

With men on first and second, the first baseman plays off the bag but not as far to his right as if there were no runners on base. This is with one or two out and no bunt anticipated. If it is a bunt situation, the first baseman plays on the inside corner of the bag and charges the plate as the ball is pitched, precisely as if there were a runner only on first.

When there is a bunt with men on first and second, the first baseman, especially if he is left-handed, is afforded a golden opportunity to break the back of the rally by turning the bunt into a force-out at third. The Giants in 1936 and 1937 were particularly good at this play.

Their success in making it depended upon several factors, the most important of which was the shortstop's playing almost on second base to keep the runner from getting a jump on the play. The second vital factor was the fielding skill of the pitcher, who would break to his right from the rubber as soon as the ball was pitched, so as to be in position to field a ball bunted toward third. The first baseman would charge in and to his right, to protect against balls bunted directly through the pitcher's box. The second baseman covered first, the third baseman played on the bag, unless the ball was bunted directly at him.

There were only two ways to overcome this defense, both of them difficult. One was to have the batter hit away, a risky procedure which might easily wind up in a double play. The other was to have the batter bunt directly down the first-base line, since Terry, breaking to cover the unprotected area around the pitcher's box, was forced to leave this territory unguarded. It takes an excellent bunter to bunt directly down either base line.

Since the purpose of the first baseman's holding a runner on base is primarily in the hope that the pitcher may pick him off, there should be a few words on the procedure of the first baseman on the pick-off play. This applies only to successful pick-off throws, not bluff throws to drive the runner back to first. Only about half the time will the runner be caught coming back to first on a pick-off, in which case, of course, the first baseman's duty is merely to put the ball on him. The rest of the time the runner will be caught either leading or breaking toward second.

When the runner is trapped off base, the first baseman should start toward him immediately, forcing him to break into a run and giving him no time to jockey. Then he should get the ball to the man covering second. Having made the throw, the first baseman should continue toward second, following the runner. Don't worry about first base. That will be covered either by the pitcher or the catcher. Sometimes the second baseman circles behind to cover first, and even the right fielder can come in to cover the bag.

The purpose of following the runner to second is plain. If,

seeing the ball has beaten him to second, he attempts to retreat, the first baseman is right behind him, which makes for a shorter throw and leaves the runner less space in which to jockey around.

Frequently a runner is picked off first when there is another runner on third. It is here that hesitation is fatal to a first baseman. As soon as he receives the ball from the pitcher, he must take a quick glance at the man on third to determine if he can be picked off by a snap throw to the third baseman or if he has broken for the plate, in which case the play is made to the catcher. If neither situation prevails, the first baseman should quickly get the ball to the shortstop covering second. Then, if the man on third breaks for home, the shortstop has the ball in plenty of time to make the play at the plate.

A first baseman is less likely to be tricked on a hit-and-run play than the shortstop or second baseman, since the play is usually directed at hitting the ball through the spot vacated by either of them as they go to cover second. Although the prospects of a hit-and-run's being employed are not as easily anticipated as those of the sacrifice bunt, the first baseman can help protect his club against the hit-and-run. First, he should know that certain opposing players are adroit at the hit-and-run and therefore may be expected to use it. Second, he can do his part by holding the runner close to first, giving him little chance to get a jump on the ball.

One play which frequently makes first baseman look awkward is a ball bunted, or topped, directly down the line. If there is a man on first, the smart batter will refuse to run out the hit, making the first baseman tag him. The batter may even retreat toward the plate. The first baseman should never be gulled into chasing the batter back to the plate. If, after fielding the ball, he sees there is no chance to get the man going to second, the thing for the first baseman to do is to straddle the line, sizing up the situation. Then he can back up and touch first, since he has the man at second under observation, or turn and toss to the second baseman, who by that time will be covering first. If he attempts to chase the backpedaling batter, he may give the man on second a chance to go to third.

Other duties are imposed upon the first baseman besides playing the bag. He must be prepared to cover home plate or second base in run-down plays, to back up outfield throws at second and sometimes at third base. And if he has a good arm, he must go into the outfield to handle the relay on long throws to the plate.

On long hits to right field, particularly with a runner on first, it is advisable for the first baseman to go across the diamond to a spot on the left-field side of the pitcher's mound, so he will be in a position to cut off the throw of the right fielder to third base. Then, if the throw has no chance of nailing the man going from first to third, the first baseman can intercept it and frequently nail the batter, who has rounded first and is on his way to second. Dolph Camilli of the Dodgers and Long George Kelly of the Giants were particularly valuable for their work on cutoffs and relays of outfield throws.

Next to the catcher, the first baseman probably has more chances to give the pitcher a word of encouragement than any other player. Since he has the ball so frequently, after put-outs and throws to first base, he can walk over to the mound and steady the pitcher. This is important in the case of certain pitchers who are inclined to work too fast when under pressure.

Fans always wonder what the conversation is about in these conferences at the mound. According to the Yankee legends, the following took place in the first game of the 1932 World Series at Yankee Stadium with the Cubs. The Yanks were off in front about midway in the game when Red Ruffing, known as a cool pitcher under fire, appeared to lose control. He walked one hitter and got three balls and no strikes on the next. Lou Gehrig, an intense competitor, called time and walked over from first base.

Gehrig asked Red, "Are you sure you're all right, Red? Remember, now, this is a World Series!"

Ruffing said, "I'm all right, Lou. By the way, what town are we in?"

Both laughed and the pressure was off.

Traditionally, players at certain positions are supposed to be capable of hitting the long ball. In the chapter on batting we will discuss that in detail. The first baseman is one of those who is called on to pull his weight at bat. Once upon a time there may have been a question of whether it was better to have at first a smooth fielder who wasn't much of a hitter or a powerhouse player who was clumsy around the bag. If a manager is forced to choose between a first baseman with fielding skill and one with power, he will take the powerhouse every time.

When Bill Terry, not only a wonderful fielder but one of the very few batters to achieve a season's average of .400 in modern times, came to the end of his playing days, the Giants had a real job to find a successor. One of those they were considering was a powerhouse hitter but a sieve as a fielder.

John Kieran, the "Information Please" genius, then a sports columnist on the *New York Times*, was discussing him with a real Giant fan.

"The guy'll hit a million home runs," the fan exclaimed.

"Yes, but who'll field all the balls he misses?" Kieran asked.

"Mel Ott."

6: The Second Baseman

A SECOND BASEMAN must be able to throw from any position. Mere strength of arm is not enough. He must be able to get the ball away, and accurately, whether he is standing still, on the dead run, lying flat on the ground, or falling after being bumped by the runner in a force play at the base. He cannot take time to get set—while the second baseman gets set the runner gets safe.

There are three plays, all stressing unusual throwing ability, which distinguish the star from the run-of-the-mill second baseman: the underhand snap throw while on the dead run; playing the ball hit deep and hard to his left; and the play on the ball hit directly over second.

On balls hit directly to him, or not far to either side, any experienced fielder can handle the play in fairly routine fashion. It is the second baseman who can cut off base hits, not the man who plays his position on a dime, who is a real asset to his team.

Get the setup of the infield well in mind. The first baseman, most of whose throws are to his right side, is usually left-handed. For the second baseman, the shortstop, and the third baseman, most throws are to their left side. They must be right-handed. In his normal position the second baseman is a few steps to the first-base side of second.

The batter hits a slow roller or tops the ball between first base and the pitcher's mound. The second baseman comes charging in, grabs the ball while going at top speed. The batter is racing the 90 feet from the plate to first. The only way the fielder can get the ball there ahead of him is to flip it across with an underhand snap without slackening his speed.

For the fan it is one of the prettiest plays in baseball. For the second baseman's manager it is a strong indication that he has a star fielder on his team.

Difficult as this play may be, there are many who say that the acid test of a second baseman's fielding skill comes on the ball hit hard and deep to his left. On this play he makes the stop as he races away from the diamond, usually out onto the grass. Having grabbed the ball, he must turn immediately, pivoting on his right foot, and throw to first.

On a ball hit directly over the bag, he must again pivot quickly on his right foot and get the ball to first. On this play he is in a much better position to make the throw quickly, but the throw is far longer than on a ball hit to his left.

No second baseman is adequate at his position unless he can do his job well on double plays. In these he has two distinct chores. One is as the fielder who starts a double play. The other is as the pivot man.

Take the double play he starts. A man is on first; the batter hits one through the infield. The second baseman takes the ball, throws it to second, which is covered by the shortstop, who relays it to first. This means that the ball must travel from the plate to the fielder to second to first before the batter can sprint 90 feet.

The second baseman must feed the ball to the shortstop the same way all the time. The speed and split-second timing, all-important to the successful execution of the double play, are bound up in this fact.

The throw to the shortstop should always be about at his left shoulder, so that he has only to put up his glove (which is on his left hand), grab the ball as he runs, step on second and come across the bag a stride to complete the relay to first. If the shortstop knows exactly where he will receive the throw from the second baseman on all force plays at second base, his part is greatly simplified.

With the ball fed to him thus, the rest of the play is almost automatic for the shortstop. He doesn't have to look for the base and he comes in with the play unfolding before him. He loses no speed and is in the correct position to throw around the runner.

A second baseman who feeds the ball high one time and low the next upsets the best shortstop. It's bad enough that he has to lose time bending for a low throw while he locates the bag, but if he isn't confident that the ball is coming to the spot at which he expects it, he cannot commit himself.

When the second baseman acts as the pivot man on the double play, that is, when he is the man who makes the throw to first, he has two cardinal rules to remember. The first is to fire the ball hard to first base. This may seem to be so apparent that it deserves no mention, but it is neglected so frequently, and in the major leagues too, that it should be emphasized. The thrower must get something on the ball if it is going to reach first base ahead of the batter.

The next important rule for the second baseman when he acts as pivot man on a double play is to keep out of the runner's way. Here is the setup on this play: if the second baseman is covering second, that usually means that the ball has been hit to the third-base side of the infield and is taken either by the shortstop or the third baseman. The second baseman, as he takes the throw, has his back to first base. He pivots off his right foot and throws to first as he strides with his left inside the base line taking himself out of the runner's path.

It is important to avoid a crash with a runner, for he is tearing in and sliding hard with the sole intention of breaking up the double play, and the picture is complete. Some runners coming into second throw a rolling block that would make a football coach happy, as they try to upend the pivot man and make it impossible for him to throw to first.

Among modern second basemen, Charley Gehringer of the Tigers, now retired, Joe Gordon of the Yankees and the Indians, Billy Herman of the Cubs, Dodgers, and Braves are among the best on the double-play pivot. Their technique is to come across the front of the bag, on the pitcher's side, and pivot simultaneously to make the throw to first.

What made them stand out over other second basemen was that they pivoted and threw *at the same time* that they crossed the bag, not *after* they crossed it, and the fraction of a second thus saved often meant the difference between success and failure in completing a double play.

This is what the Gehringer-Gordon-Herman technique demands: The second baseman charges across so that his right foot hits the forward point of the bag, the point facing the pitcher's mound. As his foot touches the bag he pivots off it toward first base and steps away from the bag as he throws. The step-away takes him out of the runner's path. This kind of pivot and throw is nothing for a man with rheumatism to try.

Both phases of the double play—feeding the ball and pivoting—require hours and hours of practice to perfect. It is a technique that can be improved and polished by practice. There are, however, men in the major leagues today who haven't mastered it yet. It is not easy, but its value is so great that the practice it requires is an unquestionably good investment. Anybody who saw Lou Boudreau and Joe Gordon in the middle of the Cleveland infield can appreciate what can be done with the pivot when a good shortstop and second baseman operate in perfect teamwork.

Make the first one sure is a double-play law that precedes all others in importance. Too often the infielder who tries to start a double play will feed the ball sloppily in his hurry, with the result that not only is the runner safe at second but also at first. The pivot man may have to pull his foot off the bag, or miss the throw entirely, or make the catch in such an awkward position that the ball is knocked loose in a collision with the runner.

There are hundreds of double plays missed in the major

SECOND BASEMAN, PIVOTING TO THROW TO FIRST ON DOUBLE PLAY, MUST STEP OFF TOWARD THE MOUND TO AVOID A CRASH WITH THE RUNNER.

leagues every year because the man starting them has failed to make certain of the first one.

Veterans, especially, like to get the ball well in advance of the play when they are the pivot. This enables them to find the bag, avoid collisions, and puts less strain on an aging arm in completing the whip-like relay to first base. The pivot man's desire to get the ball in a hurry is reasonable enough, but the fielder who starts the double play shouldn't let his haste force him into making a bad throw, thus blowing both put-outs.

There is a double play which confuses the fans and often the players themselves. The first out is made on the batter, at first base, and the double play is completed at second, where the runner is retired. Once the batter is put out at first it is no longer a force-out at second, and the runner coming into second must be tagged with the ball.

Here is another double-play situation. A runner is on first, and the batter hits a hard one directly to the second baseman. He fields the ball at the instant the runner comes abreast of him. The second baseman has to tag the runner and fire the ball to first in time to get the hitter.

In such a setup the second baseman has to remember to keep several things in mind. He may make a swipe at the runner, graze his uniform and then throw to first. The umpire may miss the swipe variety, so make the tag emphatic. In making a vigorous tag the fielder accomplishes one of two things. Either he tags the runner so plainly that nobody can doubt it, or he pushes him so far out of the base line that the umpire has to call him out.

Again in situations of this type the runner from first may stop dead in the base path, forcing the second baseman to chase him for the put-out. The fielder must not waste time chasing the runner but has to make up his mind at once whether it is better to throw to first base or to second to make a double play, at the same time remembering that the principal thing is to keep the runner from advancing. The fielder has two "ifs" to think about.

If it is obvious that the batter can beat a relay from second base, the fielder throws to first—*if* this allows time to get the ball to second ahead of the runner. If there is time to complete the double play by making the throw to second, he makes the play that way.

When the situation comes up with runners on first and third, the second baseman's problem is even harder. In this setup the runner on third is the chief consideration. It is his chance of scoring that decides for the second baseman, who must determine whether the double play may be made without giving up a run.

Helpful as practice may be in improving a feeder or pivot man, there is one basic skill that no amount of practice seems to produce. That is the knack of whipping the arm straight across the body on double-play throws to first. Rogers Hornsby had it. Without shifting his feet or turning his body he could sidearm the ball to first with speed and accuracy. In the last twenty years the player with the nearest approach to this attribute of Hornsby's was Eddie Basinski, who played briefly with Brooklyn and Pittsburgh and never became a star or even a major-league regular.

In practicing shortstop-second baseman teamwork, each fielder must learn the other's specific style on handling the play. All fielders do not make the pivot in the same manner. Some shortstops, such as Eddie Miller, who throw as soon as they touch the base, like to get the ball well before they reach the bag. Others, such as Phil Rizzuto, come across the bag before they make the throw. But all second basemen can count on all shortstops' wanting to have the ball fed to them in the same spot every time, and that spot is shoulder-high on the left side.

Among the second baseman's numerous duties on some clubs is relaying to the right fielder, and sometimes to the center fielder, the signal for the pitch, whether it is to be a curve ball or a fast one. All he has to do is to take the catcher's sign and signal it on to the outfielders with his fingers behind his back. I don't approve, as such signs could easily be stolen by the opposition.

Knowing whether the pitch will be a curve ball or a fast ball is valuable not only to the outfielders but also to the second baseman in playing position. For instance, if a left-hander is at bat and is being curved, there is more of a chance that he will pull the ball to right field than if the pitch is a fast one. Thus the second baseman has an idea which way to be ready to break, but he must be careful never to tip off the batter by moving too soon in the direction he thinks the ball will be hit.

A second baseman who can snag Texas leaguers, those drooping fly balls that fall in no man's land between infield and outfield, is worth his weight in gold; and it is on this play that he depends on the cooperation of his teammates to prevent not only an error but physical damage.

When a second baseman goes for a Texas leaguer his only rule is to go backward as far as he can and as fast as he can, keeping his eye on the sailing ball. Since he can see nothing in the ball park except the ball itself, he has to depend on the outfielder, who is facing the play, or one of the other infielders to shout him off if there is danger of a collision. Once, however, he sees that he can get under the ball, it is up to him to call for it at the top of his lungs.

On a fly hit to right field, the second baseman should take off in that direction. The movements of the right fielder will tell him almost instantly whether it is hit short or deep. If it looks like either a deep catch or a safe hit, the second baseman must get out there to be ready to relay the outfielder's throw.

On extra-base hits to right or right center, the second baseman must line up the outfielder's throw. His knowledge of the outfielder's arm will tell him how far to go into the outfield, but in no circumstances should he get too deep to make a strong and accurate throw to third base or the plate. Only the outfielder's throw should be long.

When the ball is hit to left, and the shortstop goes into the outfield, the second baseman must move over to cover second for a possible throw. If he sees that the shortstop is coming back to cover second it is the second baseman's job to back him up. And in backing up any play, whether a peg from the outfield or a throw from the catcher on an attempted steal, the backer-up must be sure to place himself at least 10 feet behind the man for whom the ball is intended. If the throw is missed by the first man his body will obscure it from the backer-up playing too close in. Moreover, the backer-up breathing on the first fielder's neck will have no chance to recover a ball that caroms off or is deflected.

To any player on defense, knowledge of the hitters is essential. It saves him countless steps and in the case of a second baseman often enables him to be in front of the ball. The business of knowing where to play the hitters is evident in veterans, but there is no reason why a player has to be around for years before he can master it. Just study the hitters and see where they generally poke various types of pitches.

Charley Gehringer and Tony Lazzeri could read the hitters like fortunetellers. Even toward the end of his career with Detroit, when he had slowed up to a marked degree, Charley was in front of every ball hit to second base. He seemed to be all over the field without having to run.

In a single inning of a game against the Yankees he put on a demonstration of his knowledge of hitters that gave our bench the miseries. Bill Dickey slammed one down toward right field. Gehringer was waiting there to toss him out. Bill Johnson, next up, slashed one through the box, almost over second base. Gehringer was waiting there to toss him out. On the bench Lefty Gomez moaned, "Look at that sucker; he's playing second base by ear."

One habit a second baseman should attempt to develop, since it is a valuable aid no matter what play comes up, is to be in motion as the pitcher delivers the ball. Joe Gordon is a master of this art. He always weaves with the windup, coming forward on his toes as the ball is pitched. Thus he is never caught flat-footed and is constantly in a position to break with the ball. Being caught flat-footed means exactly what it says. A man can start more quickly from his toes than from his arches.

Here is a play that calls for exact judgment by the second baseman and pays dividends to experience: There are runners on first and third, one or none out, the score is close. The usual infield alignment has the first baseman and third baseman in on the grass to cut off the run. The second baseman and the short-stop are halfway in, close enough to make a play at the plate but deep enough to take advantage of a double-play possibility.

The second baseman has to have all the possibilities clearly in his mind before the ball is hit to him, so that he does not have to stand around scratching his head about what to do with it, but makes the play automatically.

The thing that the defense wants most is to make the double play, while keeping the run from scoring. If it were merely a matter of cutting off the run at the plate, all four infielders would be playing in on the grass, ignoring the double-play pos-sibilities entirely.

The second baseman must know the speed of the batter and of the runners on first and third. Since he is playing halfway in, he will be unable to get any reasonably hard-hit ball that goes more than a step or two to his right or left. If it is a slow roller he will have little chance of making a double play.

When the second baseman plays in close to cut off a run he should keep his throws to the third-base side of the catcher, not so far up the line as to bring him away from the plate, but to a spot at which the catcher can be waiting to put the ball on the runner before he reaches the plate. A throw to the first-base side not only is awkward for the catcher to handle, since it comes to his bare-hand side, but it pulls him back from the plate he is trying to protect and gives the runner an easy chance to slide away from the tag.

A second baseman varies his position according to the situation. With a man on first base and a bunt anticipated, the second baseman has to be ready to break to his left because there is a strong chance that he will have to cover first on the bunt. Out of this situation, there may also develop a "trap play," in which the pitcher pitches out and the second baseman comes in behind the runner to take a snap throw from the catcher for a pick-off. The runner, expecting a bunt and lured into taking a lead because the first baseman is playing in, usually breaks on the pitcher's motion, which leaves him helpless if the play is a pitch-out.

The general rule on covering second on attempted steals is that the shortstop covers when the steal develops out of a bunt play, and also when the batter is left-handed. The second baseman covers when the batter is right-handed. This rule, of course, is only general and does not always hold. When the batter has a reputation as an adroit manipulator of the hit-and-run and can hit "behind the runner," that is, to right field, the shortstop will cover regardless of whether the batter hits from right or left.

Some of the better base runners often bluff steals as the ball is being pitched in an effort to learn in advance whether the bag will be covered by the second baseman or shortstop. This information helps them to decide what type of slide to adopt and it also helps the batter if the hit-and-run is on, because he knows which infielder will go over to cover and therefore where the "hole" will be. The second baseman should be on the alert against tipping off the opposition that he will be covering on a steal.

The teamwork of second baseman and shortstop is as essential on attempts to pick the runner off second as it is on double plays. It is the duty of both to make bluffs at the bag so as to reduce the lead of the runner and to alternate these bluffs so as to distract the runner by forcing him to watch both fielders at once. A runner who isn't certain whether the shortstop or the second baseman will attempt to pick him off will be forced to shorten his lead. Because the runner has the second baseman within sight all the time, there is less chance of the second baseman's making the pick-off, but sometimes he can divert the runner's attention sufficiently to enable the shortstop to make a dash for the bag.

The job of the second baseman on double steals follows the pattern of his assignment on a steal by only one runner. If the batter is a left-handed pull-hitter the shortstop covers second, and the second baseman stays in position until the ball is pitched and then moves in to the cutoff position. If the batter is a right-handed pull-hitter the second baseman goes directly to cover second as the ball is pitched.

When the defense calls for a pitch-out in an attempt to break up a double steal, the infielders can leave their positions at once because there is little possibility that the batter will hit, but they must be sure not to break before the pitch and tip off the other side that a pitch-out is coming up.

The double steal has almost disappeared since the advent of the lively ball. Now, with men on first and third, the runner on first may occasionally break for second with the hope of eliminating the double-play possibilities, but the runner on third only rarely collaborates with him in breaking for the plate.

Because of the scarcity of attempted double steals, the cutoff defense against them, using two men, is rarely used any more. The popular defense now is to have either the second baseman, or the shortstop, play in front of the bag, ready to charge the ball if the runner on third breaks for home.

Assuming that the second baseman has moved into the position for the cutoff, he is again in a spot in which he must depend upon his judgment and experience. He must determine from the actions of the runner on third whether to allow the throw to go through or to cut it off. If the runner on third has broken for the plate, the second baseman intercepts the catch-

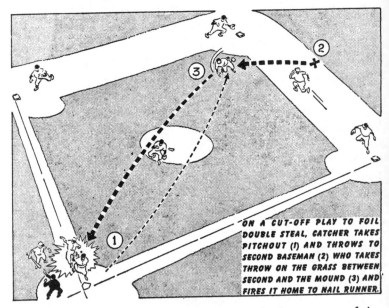

ON A CUT-OFF PLAY TO FOIL DOUBLE STEAL, CATCHER TAKES PITCHOUT (1) AND THROWS TO SECOND BASEMAN (2) WHO TAKES THROW ON THE GRASS BETWEEN SECOND AND THE MOUND (3) AND FIRES IT HOME TO NAIL RUNNER.

er's throw and fires it to the plate. Otherwise he gets out of the way and allows it to go through to the shortstop covering the bag.

There will be occasions after the second baseman has cut off the throw when the runner on third will head back to base. Then the second baseman must wheel to see if anything can be done to prevent the other runner from reaching second.

The important thing for the second baseman to decide when acting as the cutoff man against the double steal is to determine whether the break for the plate by the runner at third is the real thing or merely a feint. He shouldn't be too eager to cut off the throw, because this almost assures the runner on first of reaching second. Experience and judgment are the factors which will enable him to determine whether he should cut off the throw or allow it to go through.

If, on the double-steal defense, the second baseman is not the cutoff man but is playing back to cover the bag, his alertness can help the play. The man playing deeper can have both runners under observation, while the cutoff man can watch only the runner on third. It is up to the man covering the bag to shout instructions to the cutoff man.

The man covering the base on all steals should have the bag between his feet to leave only one opening, for the runner may slide. If the runner can slide for only one side of the bag, the second baseman has only that one spot which he must protect with his tag. Make tags with the gloved hand, and grab the ball firmly so the runner can't kick or knock it out of the glove. Occasionally the ball will get there well ahead of the runner, so that the tag can be made with a two-handed grip, but usually it is a one-handed tag, and it is up to the fielder to see that he doesn't lose possession of the ball.

In covering second on a double steal the fielder has to take extra precautions not to get tangled up with the runner, which would let the man on third break for the plate. As soon as the tag is made the infielder should come off the bag and in onto the diamond, ready to throw to the plate or to third.

On rare occasions the pitcher is used as the cutoff man against double steals. Charley Dressen tried this defense once when he was managing Cincinnati and never tried it again.

This is how Dressen describes the play: "We were playing the Cubs, and they had men on first and third. Kiki Cuyler was the man on third and in those days Kiki was full of run.

Ernie Lombardi was our catcher, and I sensed an attempted double steal and gave Ernie the cutoff sign to give the pitcher.

"This sign was merely Lombardi folding the fingers of his right hand over the end of his catcher's mitt. The pitcher was then to intercept his throw and shoot it back to the plate. Ernie gave the sign and Cuyler broke for the plate. Big Lom whipped the ball to the pitcher. The pitcher ducked and let it go through to second base. Alex Kampouris made a great catch and fired it back to Lombardi. This was the throw that the pitcher cut off."

7: Third Base

IT is a baseball axiom that third basemen are made, not born. A check of most of the players covering the far turn in the majors will show that they started their baseball careers at another infield position, usually shortstop. Finding that they lacked the necessary speed and agility to range as a shortstop should, they were moved by some manager or another to third.

This isn't to imply that third base is a haven for worn-out shortstops. Although Joe McCarthy is supposed to have said once that you could play third base in a rocking chair, Joe always managed to have a pretty good man covering the bag for him on his clubs. Some truly great ballplayers have been third basemen, fellows like Ken Keltner of Cleveland, Pie Traynor of the Pirates, and George Kell of Detroit.

A case in favor of the manufactured third baseman is that of Bob Elliott of the Boston Braves, who was voted the National League's most valuable player for 1947. It was Frankie Frisch, as manager at Pittsburgh, who turned Elliott into a third baseman after Bob had been playing the outfield for a half-dozen seasons. Incidentally, Frisch himself was a transplanted infielder, having joined the Giants as a third baseman and then switching to second base, where he gained his greatest fame.

Elliott was twenty-five years old when Frisch sold him a bill of goods on third base. Bob had played three seasons in the outfield for the Pirates, but Frisch was in dire straits for a third baseman, and Elliott seemed to him ideal conversion material.

"I could practically go out right now and play third, it's that easy," Frisch argued, "and I'm way over forty. You don't have a darn thing to do out there. Give it a try, Bob. It'll add years to your baseball life, and you won't be wearing yourself out as you are now, running around the outfield."

It happened that in Elliott's first game at third, the opposing club was murdering the ball. Line drives were whistling by him, bouncing off his chest, and he was diving into the dirt after balls. Finally one particularly tough smash flattened him, caroming off his chest so hard that the pitcher was able to grab the ball and throw the batter out at first.

"Add years to my life, eh!" the prostrate Elliott roared to Frisch, in on the Pirate bench. "I'm practically dead already and I've only been out here an hour!"

Elliott's experience at third that day was unusual, to say the least. A third baseman does not get nearly as many fielding chances as the other infielders. It is for this reason that the third baseman must carry some lumber to the plate with him. He is expected to be not only a consistent hitter but a long-ball hitter.

The hardest play for the third baseman is the misnamed "swinging bunt," which is not a bunt at all but a topped ball at which the batter has taken his full cut and which trickles to the infield. The third baseman does not get a jump on this ball as he would on a bunted ball which he anticipated. Because the batter is taking his full cut, the third baseman is playing deep.

There is only one way for the third baseman to play the swinging bunt. He must charge the ball, field it barehanded and throw to first almost with the same motion. The important thing here is for the third baseman to keep his eye on the ball and not lift his head until he has grabbed it. Very often a third baseman will charge one of these swinging bunts and miss the ball completely with his bare hand. When that happens, it is fairly certain that he has taken his eye off the ball.

Most of the fielding chances offered a third baseman are either slow-hit balls, such as bunts or swinging bunts, or hard smashes in which he often has the ball almost before the batter has left the plate. Although he has a long throw, the third base-man doesn't necessarily require a strong arm, since on most of his long throws he has plenty of time in which to get the ball away.

One of the third baseman's greatest assets is an ability to field balls hit to his right, to protect the foul line. Balls hit down the foul line to the outfield invariably go for extra bases, so it is a big help to a pitcher if they are even knocked down, let alone fielded clean. One of the best in the business at protecting the foul line is Ken Keltner. He can backhand a ball hit down the line as skillfully as any third baseman I have ever seen. In fact, I have particular reason to remember Ken because when my hitting streak of fifty-six straight games was broken in a night game in Cleveland in 1941, he made two stops on balls I hit over the bag which I thought were sure two-baggers when they left the bat.

On plays to his left, the third baseman should range as far as possible. Once in a great while a third baseman may be un-able to make a play on a ball which the shortstop might have fielded for a put-out if the third baseman hadn't played it. This happens so infrequently that the third baseman should not per-mit it to interfere with his coverage to his left. The alley be-tween the shortstop and the third baseman must be protected and it can be protected only when the third baseman goes after every ball hit to his left.

A third baseman should be as certain on pop flies as a catcher and should be able to cover far more territory. On foul pops hit near the stands, the third baseman should sight the walls before he starts so he will know how far he can go and then set sail at once. Even if the ball is seemingly hit into, or even over, the stands, the good third baseman will give it a chase because the wind often plays funny tricks in ball parks. Good third base-men sometimes catch balls hit *INTO* the stands. The procedure here is to run to the spot at which the ball is dropping, grasp the box railing with the right hand and stretch the gloved hand as far as possible into the stands. Catches made under these circumstances give the pitcher a great lift.

It was a third baseman's alert catch of a foul pop that helped ensure a Yankee victory over the Dodgers in the opening game of the 1941 World Series. It was a highly important win, for Brooklyn took the second game; and had they won the first as well, they might have been tough to overtake.

The Dodgers scored one run in the seventh, to come within a run of a tie, and had runners on first and second with none out. Jimmy Wasdell was sent up to hit for Hugh Casey and he raised a foul toward the Yankee dugout on the third-base side of the field. Red Rolfe, playing third for us, raced for the ball, and circled so that he could make the catch facing the infield.

Peewee Reese, who was on second base, had sensed it would be a difficult catch and one which should leave Rolfe in an awkward position after making it, in all likelihood facing the stands. He tagged up at second, determined to advance on the play, and when the ball was caught he broke for third. But Rolfe had maneuvered himself into such a position that he had the play in front of him after he made the catch. He had circled to face the infield when he took the ball, a fact on which Reese hadn't figured. Nor had he figured that Phil Rizzuto, the Yankee shortstop, would break for third, too, arriving there a split second ahead of Reese, in time to take Rolfe's throw and complete the double play by tagging Peewee.

The lift that this gave Red Ruffing, the Yankee pitcher, was marvelous. Instead of only one out and runners on first and second, there were now two out and only a runner on first. And Brooklyn had its big guns coming up, too—Dixie Walker, Billy Herman, Pete Reiser, and Dolph Camilli, a pretty tough array of hitters back in 1941. When Walker grounded out, the inning was over, and Ruffing had no further trouble through the eighth and ninth.

Reese was criticized for taking this gamble, but it took super-playing by both Rolfe and Rizzuto to nail him, and had he made third, as he figured to, he would have been in a position to bring home the tying run on a fly ball or a reasonably difficult infield out.

Because pitchers generally are weak fielders, the third base-man should endeavor to catch every pop-up hit in the vicinity of the pitcher's box. Third basemen also can help out the catcher and the first baseman on pop-ups. A catcher will often "lose" a ball when he has flung off his mask, and it will be up to the third baseman to make the catch. First basemen often have trouble with pop flies hit between them and the plate be-cause in most parks right field is the sun field, and the first base-man chasing a pop-up in front of him often has to look right into the setting sun. In certain ball parks, such as Sportsman's Park in St. Louis, the setting sun coming through openings in the back of the stands can blind a player for a moment.

There are no limitations upon the amount of ground a third baseman may attempt to cover in chasing pop flies. One play re-lated to pop flies which the third baseman should never neglect is covering second base when both shortstop and second base-man are chasing a Texas leaguer hit back of second. Since both these men are in pursuit of the ball, the base is unprotected, and the batter can get himself a cheap double if the ball falls safely in the outfield, and the third baseman is not alert.

This applies to situations in which there is a man on first base, as well as when the bases are empty. The runner on first will go about halfway down the base line on such Texas leaguers, ready to hustle into second to beat the force play if the ball falls safely and ready to dash back to first to avoid being doubled if the ball is caught. If the third baseman runs down to cover second when the other two infielders are chasing the fly, he is in a position to take the throw for the force-out if the ball falls safely. He needn't worry about leaving third unprotected under these conditions, since it becomes the duty of the pitcher or catcher to cover that bag.

The third baseman has the opportunity to start many a double play and he, above all other infielders, must obey the rule to make the first out certain. With a man on first, or men on first and second, he usually starts the double play by throwing to second. Only when the ball is hit to him right on top of the base should he attempt to start the double play by stepping on third for the force-out. This force-out possibility, of course, applies only when there are men on first and second, or when the bases are filled.

The temptation to step on third is great, but the experienced third baseman avoids it and starts the double play by way of second base or, with the bases filled, by way of the catcher. There are few double plays executed by the third baseman's stepping on the base and then making the long throw across the diamond to first. It is easier to make it by way of second base. When the bases are filled the double play should be started with a throw to the plate, unless the runner on third has taken such a break that he can't be nailed. It is up to the third baseman to gauge the possibilities of this at a glance and decide whether to start the double play via the plate or via second base.

Another situation in which the third baseman's judgment must be quick and sure is on balls hit to him with runners on first and third and one out. He must decide instantly whether there is a chance to close the inning with a double play by way of second base, or whether he should play to get only the man going home from third. Here, of course, the score of the game helps determine his decision. If his team is ahead by more than one run, the proper procedure is to neglect the run going home and to keep the potential tying and winning runs off the bases.

Those who saw Pie Traynor in action say that he was the best third baseman in the business at handling a run-down between third and home. When the ball was hit to him under these conditions, he would fire it to the plate instantly and then start home after the runner. If the runner, seeing he was cut off, stopped to jockey for a run-down and thus permit the batter to reach second, he'd find Traynor right behind him to take the throw from the catcher. So adroit was Traynor at this particular maneuver that it was standard procedure for Pittsburgh to make a double play out of this situation, Traynor tagging the runner with the catcher's return throw and then throwing to second to complete the double.

A third baseman who is adept at this routine will get opportunities to benefit from it other than on balls hit to him. On ground balls hit to the second baseman on which the runner from third breaks for the plate and on which the play is to the plate, the third baseman can follow the runner right in, so as to shorten the distance of the catcher's throw if a run-down develops. Under these conditions, the shortstop must come over and cover third.

A third baseman must always be on the alert for the squeeze play with a runner on third, particularly if the batter is a skilled bunter. On the squeeze, the play is made as on a swinging bunt, the ball being fielded with the bare hand, and the throw being made from the position in which the ball is fielded. There is no time to straighten up.

The squeeze has been employed more often in recent years than it was when I first broke into the American League. This is particularly true in the National League, ever since the Dodgers won the 1941 pennant. Leo Durocher employed the squeeze play a great deal that season, and his success with it caused a general revival of the play. The Dodgers use it fre-

THIRD BASEMAN FIELDS
BUNT OR SLOW ROLLER
WITH BARE HAND AND
WHIPS IT TO FIRST IN THE
SAME MOTION.

quently with the bases filled, even though in this case the play at the plate is a force-out, and it isn't necessary for the catcher to tag the runner.

One of the situations in which Durocher employs the squeeze is novel and almost foolproof because it cannot be circumvented even by the pitch-out, which is the one usual antidote for the squeeze. This is when the bases are filled, and the count is three balls and no strikes on the batter. The Brooklyn runner on third starts with the pitcher's windup, and all the batter has to do is to bunt the ball to bring in the run. He is bound to get a good ball to bunt at, since the pitcher will be making every effort to get the ball across and avoid walking the batter and thus forcing in the run. If it is a bad ball, of course, the batter walks, and the run is forced across.

In addition to being alert for the squeeze play whenever there is a runner on third, the third baseman should be on the watch for a bunt at all times, even with two out and nobody on base. He should be on his toes with every pitched ball, moving in toward the plate unless there are two strikes on the hitter, in which case he can drop back and play deeper.

There are certain situations which demand a bunt. It is no great trick for the third baseman to anticipate these plays, since every fan in the stands knows when a sacrifice bunt is coming up. One thing the third baseman should always remember is that there is a possibility of a third-strike bunt with a sacrifice situation. This is particularly true when the batter is the pitcher. The manager often gambles with a third-strike bunt here because the average pitcher is not only a poor batter but also a slow runner and therefore a dangerous double-play risk.

With runners on first and second and none out, the sacrifice bunt is almost mandatory. Some clubs defend against this by bending every effort to make the force play at third. This is the play the Giants used to make so well when Bill Terry was playing first base for them. If the play is made to third, it is up to the third baseman to play on the bag. He must, of course, be alert for a ball bunted directly down the third-base line which the pitcher can't get off the mound in time to handle.

If the third baseman has to handle the bunt himself with runners on first and second, the force at third is, of course, eliminated. The third baseman will have a possible force at second base, where the shortstop will be covering, if the ball is bunted hard enough. Otherwise he will have to make the play at first base.

When covering third for a force-out on bunt plays of this type, the third baseman must be ready for a poor throw to him. This is particularly true if the bunt is fielded by a right-handed pitcher, since he will have to wheel to make the throw to third. It has been my observation that the majority of wild throws the third baseman is forced to handle in this situation are low throws into the dirt. The wild throw which is high or wide is exceptional. The third baseman must brace himself for the throw, since the runner will come in from second sliding hard.

On these sacrifices with runners on first and second, the third baseman and pitcher must know precisely what they are to do. Even though it has been all prearranged, the third baseman can lose nothing by walking to the mound and talking it over with the pitcher before the ball is delivered. If the pitcher knows in advance that he is to break to the third-base side and that the first baseman will come in to cover from that side, there should be no slip-up. The third baseman then will know that it is his duty to field only such bunts as are so far to the pitcher's right and so close to the third-base line that the pitcher has no chance to make the play.

The importance of the pitcher's and third baseman's working together in such a situation can't be stressed too much. Quite often, even in the major leagues, the third baseman and pitcher will collide on such bunts, or the pitcher will field the ball with the third baseman practically at his elbow and nobody covering third.

Although the shortstop ordinarily will handle relay throws from the outfield on balls hit to left or left-center, there are certain outfield plays in which the third baseman must go out into the outfield to take the relay, such as when the ball is hit directly down the left-field line. Also in some ball parks the stands near the left-field foul line may jut out in such a way as to form a pocket. The left fielder, after retrieving the ball, will need assistance from the third baseman to take the relay, since his vision will be obscured. In such cases, the third baseman should go 50 or 60 feet into left field to take the throw, but not so deep that he can't make a quick and accurate throw to the plate or to second base if required. In such circumstances, the shortstop will come over and cover third.

On hits into right and right-center, in which the second baseman goes out to take the relay, the shortstop covers second base and should be backed up by the third baseman. In backing up in these cases the third baseman should play at least 15 or 25 feet behind the shortstop on a direct line with the shortstop and the thrower.

There is a bit of automatic backing up required of the third baseman when the pitcher throws to first base in an effort to pick off the runner. As the first baseman returns the throw to the pitcher, the third baseman should back him up in case the toss gets by him. Probably no one has ever seen a pitcher miss this return throw from the first baseman, nor the third baseman fail to go over and back up the pitcher—just in case.

It is very rare indeed that a runner is picked off third by a pitcher, except on a planned play, yet it is the duty of the third baseman to hold the runner as close to the bag as possible by making feints in his direction. The purpose of these feints is to keep the runner from getting a break for the plate on balls hit to the infield. If the third baseman can keep the runner worried, forcing him to make breaks back toward third, he will cut a couple of strides from the latter's efficiency and possibly make the difference between his being safe or out at the plate.

On those rare occasions when a runner is picked off third it is usually by a snap throw from the catcher, which means that the third baseman must be able to get back to the bag quickly to make the play. Sometimes there is a set, prearranged play for this, in which the ball is pitched out. The Braves, when Casey Stengel was managing the club, had a trick play for this, which depended upon the batter's being right-handed. The pitcher threw directly at the batter's head, yelling a warning as he did so. The batter, of course, hit the ground. It was Stengel's theory that there was something about a batter's biting the dust which caused all other players to freeze involuntarily. The catcher, taking this simulated dust-off throw on the third-base side of the plate, then threw to third when the base runner, according to the Stengel theory, had "frozen" off the bag.

"I finally had to discard the play," related Casey, "because the fellow I had playing third used to 'freeze' along with the base runner, and it used to keep our left fielder busy all afternoon running down the catcher's throws in the bull pen."

The hidden-ball play is a play which isn't worked very frequently but is pulled more often by third basemen than by any other infielder.

There is no excuse for any base runner's being picked off with the hidden-ball trick. And he shouldn't try to alibi himself by blaming it on the coach. All a base runner has to do to protect himself against the hidden-ball play is to keep his foot on the base he is occupying until the pitcher puts his foot on the rubber. If the pitcher puts his foot on the rubber without the ball in his possession, he is guilty of a balk.

Simple as this precaution against the hidden ball is, there are a couple of major-leaguers caught off base through its use every year. Babe Pinelli, a National League umpire, was one of the best of hidden-ball fakers, when he was third baseman of the Cincinnati Reds.

"I used to walk out to talk to the pitcher with the ball in my right hand, in plain view of the runners, coaches, and everybody," explained Pinelli. "I'd keep chunking the ball into my glove in that nervous way you've seen all infielders handle a ball during a time out. I'd be doing this while I was talking to the pitcher. Then I'd take my bare hand, without the ball, and place it in the pitcher's glove, as though I were giving him the ball. I'd conceal the ball in my gloved hand by making a fist of my glove.

"The success of the play from there on depended upon the pitcher. It was up to him to keep his gloved hand close to his side as though he had the ball in it and putter around behind the mound, rubbing his bare hand in the dirt, kicking the ground with his spikes, any sort of movement which would attract the runner's attention. Then, if the runner stepped off the base, I had him.

"Once, playing against Brooklyn, I picked a runner off second with the hidden ball, even though I was playing third at the time. Sammy Bohne was playing second for Cincinnati. I had the ball hidden, and the runner came about 6 feet off second base, watching the shortstop. Bohne moved over and got on the bag. I whipped the ball to him and it landed in his glove with a snap like a rifle shot. In fact, it must have sounded exactly like a shot because the runner toppled over backwards right in his tracks, without making any effort to get back on the base. All Bohne had to do was walk over and tag him. When the runner got back to the Brooklyn bench, Uncle Wilbert Robinson, the manager, yelled, 'What happened out there?'

" 'I thought I was shot,' confessed the runner.

" 'You should have been,' said Robbie."

8: The Shortstop

THE SUREST measure of a baseball team is its strength down the middle. Draw a line right down the middle of a baseball field, from home plate across second base and on to the outfield; the players along that line—catcher, pitcher, keystone combination, center fielder—are not only the majority of the team, but also the players who handle, in their respective zones, the greatest number of fielding chances. A team strong in all those positions is certain to be a pennant contender.

Few teams have won the pennant without a first-rate shortstop, and for those few the going must surely have been rugged. The better the shortstop, the better the team's chances to finish on top, as, for example, the Cardinals with Marty Marion and the Yankees with Frankie Crosetti.

A perfect example of the effect of a good shortstop on a team's performance is found in the Philadelphia Athletics of 1947. The Athletics, in the preseason dope stories, were almost a unanimous choice to finish in the American League cellar. They wound up in the first division, largely because of the great play of shortstop Eddie Joost, who came back from retirement. He broke no batting records, didn't even threaten them, but he covered the shortfield like a tarpaulin and sopped up every ball in sight.

Except for the pitcher, the shortstop is the one man on the team for whom real defensive skill can more than make up for a weak bat. When a shortstop comes along who is not only a great fielder but a power hitter, such as Lou Boudreau of Cleveland, there is really a star. But while a good fielding but weak hitting shortstop can stay in the regular line-up, the shortstop who is an uncertain fielder has to be better than good at bat if he is to be a first-stringer.

When Joe Cronin of the Red Sox started to slow up in the field his regular presence in the line-up continued to be justified because he was an exceptional hitter. Even so, Joe was always looking around for a successor and thinking of moving himself to third base or the outfield. His arm was still strong and his bat was always dangerous, but he knew that if he could no longer cover ground he was hurting his club by playing short.

In July, 1939, Cronin brought his team to the Yankee Stadium for a five-game series. The Yankees had a big lead in the league standings, but the Red Sox cut it in half—they won all five games. Soon afterward a newspaperman in Detroit asked Yankee manager Joe McCarthy what had happened. Joe made this explanation, off the record: "Every time we hit a ball to shortstop with men on base it was right at Cronin. He didn't have to move for a ball. A little bit to either side and these balls would have been base hits, because Joe can't get over ground any more."

Only the first baseman handles more chances than the shortstop, and at that most of the first baseman's chances are fed to him. The shortstop roams far and wide for his chances, and his duties are numerous enough to keep him busier than a one-armed paper hanger.

Above all players he must be fast of foot, strong of arm, acrobatic as a trapeze artist. He must throw hard and far, overhand, sidearm, underhand. He must make his pegs while running, falling, skidding, from a crouch, even while in the air—with both feet off the ground. He must hold the runner close to second, act as cutoff man in double-steal defenses, handle most outfield relays, line up throws from outfielder to base, go after pop flies all the way from the third-base stands to the outfield, and act as the "holler guy," the inspirational spark plug of the defensive team.

In this book we have talked chiefly about where the fielder should go to get the ball and what he should do with it after he gets it. *Getting* the ball, the actual fielding of a hit or thrown ball, is something that cannot be mastered by reading any set

GET IN FRONT OF BALL
...FEET CLOSE TOGETH-
ER (WHEN POSSIBLE)...
GLOVED HAND ALMOST
FLAT ON GROUND.

of instructions. Skill at fielding is developed by applying long practice to natural talent.

There are, however, certain correct ways to take ground balls and fly balls which may be described with benefit to a young player, and there is no more logical place to describe them than in connection with the shortstop, who fields everything.

Field a ground ball with the back of the gloved hand almost

flat on the ground and both hands close together, so that the bare hand can come over on top of the ball the instant it hits the glove. Occasionally a fielder will have to field the ball with the gloved hand alone, but two hands should be used whenever possible.

Try to get *in front* of every ball; do not field it from the side if you can possibly get in front of it. Hold your feet close together to block the ball if it gets through your hands. Some shortstops occasionally go down on one knee to be sure the ball doesn't get by; but this is not recommended as a general practice, for it slows up the fielder in getting the ball away.

Catch pop flies away from the body. On balls caught chest-high and lower, put up your hands with the little fingers lying alongside each other. On balls caught above the chest, put up your hands with the thumbs side by side.

Some infielders employ the basket type of catch on pop flies, holding the hands together, inner sides against the stomach, and maneuvering to let the ball drop into the basket thus formed. This is not a natural way to catch a ball, and proof of it is that Johnny Rigney, the Giants' second baseman, who is a highly successful basket catcher, is the first major-leaguer to use this method since Rabbit Maranville. If you are already skillful at the basket catch, don't discard it, but if you're not using it now don't try to pick it up.

As for catching line drives, there is no such thing as a standard method, for there is no time to make preparations. The way some of those drives tear down to an infielder, his stop usually is made by an instinctive gesture of self-defense.

The importance of those *two* essentials of a good ballplayer —strong arm and swift foot—are never more apparent than in a shortstop. If he hasn't a strong arm it doesn't matter how much ground he can cover to get the ball, and if he can't cover ground to get the ball it doesn't matter how hard he could have thrown it. He must have not only the strongest arm on the team but the most versatile—for he has to throw underhand, overhand, and sidearm.

The ability of a shortstop to cover ground and throw gets its severest test on balls hit to his right—to the third-base side. Having covered a lot of ground to get the ball, he must make a long throw to first base, usually from off balance, for the right foot, from which he makes the throw, will have skidded a few inches when he has braked himself. Joe McCarthy recommends a short hop on the right foot so that the shortstop can regain his balance and get plenty of zip on the ball when he throws it. Once Phil Rizzuto had mastered this little tap-dance step he improved a hundred per cent on balls hit to his right.

Another play which calls for speed and throwing skill on the part of the shortstop is on slow hit balls which elude the fielding efforts of the pitcher, particularly those bounders which go through the box. Here the shortstop must get the ball quickly and make an underhand throw. Sometimes he will have to make what amounts to a full sidearm throw to second base for force-outs on ground balls which he has fielded deep and to his right.

Like the second baseman, the shortstop must be fast and smooth in starting and pivoting in double plays. As the pivot his task is somewhat simpler than that of the second baseman because he has the play in front of him most of the time, whereas the second baseman has to make a complete turn to relay the ball to first.

When circumstances permit, the shortstop should attempt to take the throw about a stride in advance of second base, so that he can hit the bag with his left foot, take a full stride with his right and throw. He should not worry about hitting the runner with his relay. On that subject, Frankie Crosetti says, "The only base runner I ever heard of who was hit with a shortstop's relay was Dizzy Dean in the 1934 World Series between the Cardinals and the Tigers. In the fifteen years or more that I handled relays from shortstop position I generally let the ball go right on a line for a spot between the runner's eyes and I haven't hit a base runner yet. It's just human instinct for the runner to duck, start his slide or otherwise get out of the way of a thrown ball."

The acrobatic talents of the second-base combination are particularly noticeable on double plays, in which fans frequently see the pivot man leap into the air to avoid a sliding runner and make the relay to first while still off the ground. Throwing while in mid-air is against all the accepted precepts of the game but it is done almost every day in the major leagues, although it seems to be a play which disregards the law of gravity. Joe Gordon, Peewee Reese, Marty Marion, Phil Rizzuto, and Lou Boudreau are especially good at it.

They even manage to "get something on" the throw to first, even though they haven't the advantage of balance. Usually the throw under such conditions is a snap throw, such as the catcher uses to first and third bases to pick runners off.

In double plays the shortstop should feed the ball to the pivot man at the same spot all the time, usually the left shoulder, just as the second baseman does when he starts the play. When the keystone combination perfects a smooth teamwork in feeding the ball, the danger of the pivot man's being knocked down by the runner's slide is greatly reduced, since it gives him time to get out of the way.

On all plays in which there is a runner on second, the shortstop should be alert for a chance to get him out at third. Often on a ball hit to the shortstop's extreme right, which means a long throw to first to get the batter, he can nail the runner from second with a snap throw to the third baseman. Frequently on ground balls to the infield, even ground balls on which double plays are attempted, the runner from second will swing around third to be in a position to score in the event of an error. Thus the heads-up shortstop has a chance of getting him after he has rounded third.

A shortstop who fields a ball hit to his right must make an underhand throw if he hopes to get the runner going to third. The ball must be thrown from the position in which it is fielded. This also applies to the feeding of the ball on double plays and explains why the shortstop must be able to execute a variety of throws. "He gets the ball away quickly" is real praise of a player and means that he can throw from any position.

Among his other assignments, the shortstop is the man on whom pitchers depend to keep the runner on second close to the bag. Not more than one in twenty, or even one in fifty, of the throws a pitcher makes to the shortstop picks a runner off second, but they all serve a purpose: they force the runner to hug the bag. By feinting toward second, the shortstop forces the runner to lean or even to break toward that base as the ball is pitched, which prevents him from getting a flying start on the play.

It is important to hold the runner close to second when there are runners on first and second, and a bunt play is indicated, since the smaller the lead the runner gets off second, the greater his chances of being forced at third on the bunt. It also increases the possibility of a put-out at third when there is a runner only on second, and a bunt is anticipated. This is a situation which will come up in the late innings when the first batter, representing the tying or winning run, reaches second with none out. The offensive team frequently will attempt to bunt him to third, from whence he can score on a long fly, a difficult infield chance, an error, a passed ball, or a wild pitch.

Under these conditions a shortstop sometimes will be able to pick the runner off second on a prearranged play. This is exactly what happened to the Yankees in the last game of the 1942 World Series and was a big factor in winning the championship for the Cardinals.

The Yanks were behind 4 to 2 going into the last half of the ninth. Joe Gordon singled off Johnny Beazley, and when Jimmy Brown booted Bill Dickey's grounder the tying runs were on base with none out. Tuck Stainback went in to run for Dickey, and Jerry Priddy was up to bunt the runners along.

If Priddy succeeded in bunting the runners over, the Yankees would be in a position to tie up the game with a single. Jerry went up there to do his stuff but on the first play was trapped by a planned stratagem of the Cardinals. Beazley pitched out to catcher Walker Cooper, and Marty Marion flew over to second to take a snap throw from Cooper. Gordon was picked off, and the back of the rally was broken. In fact, the World Series was over.

On this particular play, Marion had a sign from Cooper that the pitch would be wasted and he didn't make as many feints to drive Gordon back as he would ordinarily have done. Joe, of course, was trying to get as big a lead as possible, which was exactly what Marion wanted. The instant the ball left Beazley's hand, Marty raced for the bag, and there was no question about the decision. Priddy did his best to get part of his bat on the ball, even to foul it off, but it was a perfect pitch-out. And a perfect play.

On steals, the shortstop's duties are similar to those of the second baseman, as already described. The shortstop will find that steal situations are almost as easy to anticipate as bunt situations. A steal, for instance, is more likely to be attempted with two out than with none out. The speed and base-running ability of the runner on first and the pitcher's ability to hold runners on base will serve as advance information to the shortstop as to whether an attempt to steal is likely. There is more likely to be a steal attempt with a right-hander pitching than with a left-hander and more chance of an attempt against a pitcher who is not adept at holding runners on than against one who has the knack.

In covering the base against steals, the shortstop should straddle the bag, leaving only one corner exposed for the runner to come in. The tag will be made with the gloved hand most of the time and the shortstop must remember to keep a firm grip on the ball so it cannot be knocked or kicked from his glove. On a high or wide throw, the shortstop must leave the bag to field the throw, remembering that it costs less to let the runner reach second safely than to have the throw go into the outfield.

When there are runners on first and third, with the possibility of a double steal, the shortstop is less likely to find himself employed as the cutoff man than the second baseman. However, there will be occasions, particularly in the case of dead-right-field hitters, where the shortstop will have to handle all the possibilities of the attempted double steal alone.

In such circumstances, when the runner breaks from third and a cutoff is indicated, the shortstop must charge the throw from the catcher to intercept it as far in front of second base as possible, and, while still on the dead run, he must fire it to the plate. This is another of the many situations which stress the throwing power of the shortstop.

A tall, rangy shortstop is ideal, although good things can come in small packages, too, such as the Yankees' Phil Rizzuto. The taller the shortstop, the better his reach for ground balls hit to either side of him, for balls hit over his head, for wide or wild throws, etc. Also, a tall shortstop, wildly waving his arms, gives an outfielder a great target for his relay throws. In the majors, I have seen few shortstops over six feet, however.

The shortstop should handle all outfield relays on balls hit to center, left, and left-center. Because of the strong arm which his position demands, the shortstop usually is the best relay man in the infield. Once in a while there will be an exception to the rule, when a club comes up with a first baseman who has a real rifle-arm, such as George Kelly with the Giants years ago, but usually it is the shortstop who has the strongest and most accurate arm in the infield.

Sometimes on outfield hits to left, center, or left-center, the ball will go deep, and a play at third base may be indicated. When the shortstop goes into the outfield and finds that the throw does not require a relay, he can help the outfielder by getting directly between him and third base, thus lining up the throw for him.

The shortstop must remember to cover second base on all plays in which the second baseman goes into the outfield to take the relay, and to back up the second baseman on all plays in which the latter covers second and takes a direct throw from the outfield.

Just as the second baseman signals the right fielder before each pitch, the shortstop signals the left and center fielders with a finger sign. He must be careful to use his glove to hide the sign from the prying eyes of the coach on third base.

Nobody's territory is sacred to the shortstop when it comes to going after pop flies. He must go after those hit toward the pitcher's box, those which are fouled off near the stands back of third base, and all which are hit to center, left, or left-center. The farther a shortstop can range on pop flies, the greater his value to his club. A shortstop who really has talent at going back for a fly ball lets the left and center fielders play a step or two deeper, which often means the difference between an outfield put-out and a three-base hit.

Once a shortstop sees that he can't catch a pop fly, he has to shout instructions to the outfielder to make the catch. And when he finds that he can make the catch, he must be sure to yell out, warning the outfielder away. If the outfielder calls for the ball, it is up to the shortstop to give way; the outfielder will be coming in and will have the chance to make an easier catch than the shortstop with his back to the infield. The importance of yelling for the ball can't be emphasized too much. It is the only way to prevent dangerous collisions on fly balls.

While the shortstop only rarely covers third to take a throw from the outfield, he *always* covers third in run-down plays between third and home, either plays which are started by the third baseman or plays which are started anywhere else on the infield, sometimes by the shortstop himself. This frees the third baseman of the responsibility of protecting the base and enables him to dog the heels of the runner and thus abbreviate the run-down.

In all run-downs in which the shortstop himself is chasing the runner, he should follow the procedure for the other infielders, following the runner as closely as possible to shorten the distance of the return throw and cut down the runner's chances to jockey back and forth while the other runners advance.

Sometimes a shortstop will field a ball and find a runner trapped halfway between the bases, standing motionless, waiting for him to make a throw before he commits himself to a sprint toward either base. In such a case, the shortstop's best bet is to charge the runner and force him to make a break. Once a runner makes the break, the shortstop should throw to head him off, then come in behind him to take his place in the run-down.

No shortstop needs to be reminded that occasionally he will be involved in a double play at second base in which the runner must be tagged instead of just forced out. In this type of double play the first baseman makes the first out by touching the bag, then throwing to second base. The only reason for mentioning it is that it is a situation which brings countless questions from fans and leads to innumerable arguments in youngsters' games. Once the first baseman has stepped on first to retire the batter the force play is no longer in effect and the runner going into second must be tagged.

Every shortstop should remember to be loose and flexible as he fields the ball, to play the ball and never let the ball play him. That means that he should never be backing up as the ball comes to him, taking it on an awkward bound and in poor position to throw—"between hops," as the players call it.

Occasionally a shortstop turns up in the majors who is flashy but undependable. Lefty Gomez watched one Fancy Dan make every motion with a flourish. Finally a simple grounder came toward him with a couple of men on base. He muffed it completely.

"Look at him!" Gomez remarked. "He plays every hop right but the last one."

One of the greatest of modern shortstops was Dave Bancroft, and veterans of the Giants of the 1920's still talk about a play he made in a game against the Cardinals at the Polo Grounds in 1921. Its end result for Bancroft, however, was a momentous letdown.

The Giants, on their way to the first of four consecutive pennants, had a one-run lead in the top half of the ninth inning. The Cards, with one out, had three on base, and Rogers Hornsby, the finest hitter of his time, was at bat.

The question in tactics was whether to play the infield in, hoping to cut off the tying run at the plate, or to play back for the double play, which would end the game if it succeeded but which had to be executed successfully to prevent a tie score. Manager John McGraw signaled for the infield to play deep.

Hornsby hit one at a mile-a-minute clip, through the box. Although he was a right-handed hitter his power was to right-center, and Bancroft was playing him close to the bag. Taking off as the bat met the ball, Bancroft made an unbelievable stop behind the bag and with his gloved hand flipped the ball to the second baseman, who stepped on the base and fired to first in time to complete the double play and end the game.

In the clubhouse Bancroft's teammates almost tore him apart with their backslapping and handshaking congratulations. Then Mr. McGraw came in. Everyone grew quiet as he stuck out his right hand and walked over to Bancroft, who stood up and prepared to accept his manager's praise as modestly as possible.

"Shake, Banny!" McGraw commanded. "I guess I outsmarted them that time."

9: The Art of Catching

JOE DIMAGGIO, JR., was playing around on the Yankee bench before a game. He hefted bats, he glossed balls, he tried on all the baseball paraphernalia in sight, finally winding up with a catcher's mask.

"Tell your son to shed the tools of ignorance," Bill Dickey admonished. "It's a mistake ever to put 'em on—I know."

"Tools of ignorance" is standard baseball corn for mask, mitt, protector, and shin guards, the gag being that the physical duties of a catcher are so onerous that only a ballplayer who is too ignorant to play any other position would take up the job behind the plate. What makes the joke so feeble is that some of baseball's smartest players—Mickey Cochrane, Luke Sewell, Muddy Ruel, Dickey, to name very few—have been catchers.

The laborious duties, the exacting demands of catching, however, are no joke. The catcher, like the blocking back in football, is the work horse of the team. Because he is working every minute, he must be a rugged man. Generally a catcher is a big man, but there have been slim catchers who were among the best in their profession. The slim ones, however, have to be wiry and durable.

Occasionally a small man behind the mask has been more valuable to his club than a big one. A specific example was the Giants' victory in the World's Championship in 1933. It was won by catcher Gus Mancuso, although the credit went to the Big Four of the pitching staff—Carl Hubbell, Hal Schumacher, Freddie Fitzsimmons, and Roy Parmelee. All had great seasons in 1933, but all had been with the Giants the season before without being exceptionally successful.

The reason for the great improvement was the winter trade Manager Bill Terry made after the 1932 season which brought Mancuso to the Giants. The New York catching in 1932 had been handled by O'Farrell and Shanty Hogan. Both were big, heavy men. This impeded them in catching low-breaking stuff, and all four of the Giant aces relied on just such stuff—Hubbell, with his screwball; Schumacher, with his overhand sinker; Fitzsimmons, with his knuckler; and Parmelee, with his sharp-dipping curve.

Both O'Farrell and Hogan had to stoop to catch these pitches, and their bobbing as they reached for the ball robbed the pitchers of strikes. The umpire, seeing the catcher duck for the ball, was deluded into believing it was too low for the strike zone, although actually it had crossed the plate at the batter's knees. The much smaller Mancuso simply squatted on his haunches and caught these pitches in his glove without any stooping or bending, with the result that the umpire had an unobstructed view of the strike as it crossed the plate and could not question its validity. With Gus, the Big Four of the Giants were getting the strikes which were rightfully theirs.

The catcher takes his stance behind the plate with his feet about 6 inches apart, toes pointing slightly out. He squats on his haunches, balancing on the balls of his feet to make quick shifting possible.

His knees are fairly close together. He gives his signs with the fingers of his right hand under the flap of his chest protector. The right knee screens the signs from the coach and runner on first, the mitt from the coach and runner on third, as well as from the batsman, should the latter be so foolish as to take his eyes from the pitcher in an effort to steal a peek at the signs. With a runner on second, the catcher must use special care in giving his signs, using the mitt as an umbrella over his signaling.

Having given the sign, the catcher remains in his crouch to

present the best possible target to the pitcher. He rests the left forearm on his left knee, keeps his right hand inside his right leg. As the ball is about to be delivered, the catcher straightens from his crouch and spreads his feet slightly farther apart. The knees are still bent, but no more than a quarter bend; both feet are

CATCHER GIVES SIGNAL
(ABOVE) AND (RIGHT)
AWAITS THE PITCH.

flat on the ground. This is the position in which he receives the pitch.

The whole surface of the mitt, never just the tip, should be presented to the pitcher as a target. As the ball is caught in the mitt, the right hand is quickly slapped over on top of it. It is advisable to catch the ball with the left foot slightly forward, so as to be in throwing position even before the ball is delivered.

The closer a catcher stands to the plate, the better he is able to handle low pitchers. For a big man, Dickey caught very close to the hitter. This often resulted in Bill's being hit by foul tips but it paid big dividends to the Yankee pitchers. Some catchers have a tendency to catch "deep," if that's the word, because then tipped balls are deflected beyond them and there is less danger of acquiring a painful bruise. Even with all his pads, a catcher collects more bruises than anybody else on the team.

After presenting the broad side of the glove to the pitcher as a target, the catcher must readjust his hands as the ball is to be delivered. The proper way to do this is to flick the wrists up, making a cup with the palms of the hands facing each other and joined at the thumbs. This is for pitches received above the waist; for pitches below the waist the wrists are reversed, and the tips of the fingers are pointed toward the ground.

Split and broken fingers can be avoided if the catcher remembers to keep the fingers of his right hand together, and fingers and wrist thoroughly relaxed. A foul tip caroming off the bat then will merely flick the limp fingers in passing. If the hand is held stiff, the catcher is inviting a broken finger.

The catcher must shift his feet to meet the pitch. The best system is to make the first step with the foot farther away from the pitch. If the ball is outside, the catcher must shift his left foot behind his right and then take a wide stride with his right. If the ball is inside, the catcher reverses the procedure, moving his right foot first and then taking the big stride with his left. The terms "inside" and "outside" are used as they would apply if a right-handed batter were at the plate. It is just the opposite, of course, if the hitter is left-handed.

Low balls are the most difficult for a catcher to handle, and he handles them best by dropping to his knees, counting on his body to block the ball. A ball which gets by the catcher is a catastrophe. A World Series was decided on a ball which got by the catcher.

It was the missed third strike on Tommy Henrich in the

fourth game of the 1941 World Series between the Dodgers and Yankees at Ebbets Field. Had Mickey Owen, the Dodger catcher, held the ball—or even blocked it—and thrown Tommy out at first, the game would have been over, and the Series would have been tied. As it was, it got completely by

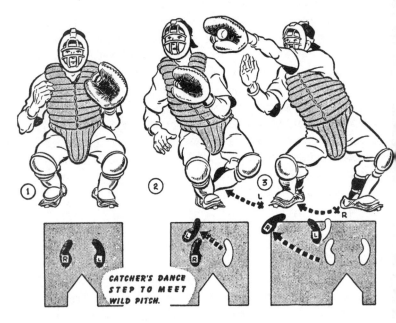

CATCHER'S DANCE STEP TO MEET WILD PITCH.

him: Henrich reached first: the Yankees scored four runs after the muff, won the game with 7 to 4 instead of losing it 4 to 3, and went on to win the Series.

It was a low, inside pitch which Henrich, a left-hander, swung at and missed. The ball was to Owen's right. He stabbed at it and it got away from him, rolling 10 or 12 feet behind him and among some policemen who had rushed onto the field, thinking the game was over.

Some thought Hugh Casey, the pitcher, had thrown a sneak

spitter, as pitchers sometimes do, and that Owen was caught un-awares by the sharp break that it took. Casey himself maintained it was just a good, sharp curve—and I believe him: because he threw me one in the fourth game of the 1947 Series six years later and made a sucker out of me.

The argument persisted about the pitch and what caused the muff until the following spring when the old catcher, Billy Meyer, then managing the Newark Bears, a Yankee farm team, told what happened. Of all the more than 30,000 people at the game, Meyer alone had a logical explanation for the error.

"Owen tried to catch the ball with his knees together," Meyer explained. "He didn't shift for the pitch."

Just as the catcher is likened to football's blocking back, he may also be compared with the quarterback in that he directs the play of the team and its strategies by calling for each pitch. He is the only player who has the entire field in front of him.

The catcher can make or break the pitcher. It is up to the catcher to pace the pitcher properly, to steady him when he is in trouble. The average pitcher, when he is being hit or is losing his control, has a tendency to pitch hurriedly. He wants to get hold of the ball as quickly as possible and fire it right back to the batter. Almost every pitcher has this tendency, and it is to curb this haste that catchers take off their masks and walk slowly out to the mound, rubbing the ball and fiddling with it before giving it back to their batterymates. Any pitcher works much better when he takes his time and deliberates before pitching.

In the big leagues the catcher is fairly familiar with the weaknesses and strength of almost every batter. He knows that spot where each batter has trouble connecting solidly and when he can be surprised by being pitched to his strength when he doesn't expect it. When a player is new to the league, the catcher usually can tell what type of hitter he is by his stance, grip, and practice swings and can work on him accordingly. Of course it takes weeks, months even, to classify a hitter accurately; but the stance, the grip, and the practice swing offer a good tip-off to the category into which the newcomer is likely to fall.

Turning foul flies into put-outs is an important duty of the man behind the plate. To muff one, especially an easy one, is almost like giving the hitter an extra time at bat, or the offensive team four outs in an inning. The first thing a catcher should do in going after a foul fly is to get rid of his mask instantly. And when he discards his mask, he should throw it as far as he possibly can, so there is no danger of stumbling over it in pursuit of the ball. Hank Gowdy stumbled over a mask in the 1924 World Series. It gave Washington an extra chance to beat the Giants.

In turning after a foul pop, the catcher should turn his body in the direction in which the pitch was delivered to the plate. If the pitch comes in on the catcher's gloved-hand side, it will be fouled off in that direction; so he should pivot to his left. If it comes in on his "meat-hand" side, he should pivot to his right.

Once having made the turn, the catcher should throw his head back to locate the ball. He should get directly under the ball and then, as it descends, back up a foot or so in order to make the catch in front of him.

Get rid of the mask at once—that's the number one rule on foul pops, for a catcher can't have full vision with a mask on. This is a good rule to follow, too, on balls which are blocked around the plate, since the mask obscures vision to the side. A catcher wearing a mask could miss completely a ball to his right or left.

There is no better rule for a catcher to follow in defending against stolen bases than to be always prepared. Expect the runner to steal on every pitch in which the base ahead of him is

open and you'll never be surprised. The catcher should anticipate a double steal whenever there are runners on first and third.

In receiving a pitch the catcher should bring his left foot forward whenever possible, to be in throwing position. The throw
is always made off the right foot, with the left foot a full stride
in front. The catcher should cock his arm and let the throw go
from alongside his right ear. A catcher who brings his arm all
the way back to throw or a catcher who steps forward with his
right foot first and then takes an extra stride with his left before
releasing the ball hasn't a chance of catching the runner.

When a runner on first breaks for second, the catcher should
make his throw on a low trajectory, so that the infielder covering the bag doesn't have to waste any time in putting the ball
on the runner by leaping for the catch. The good throw will
reach second base about a foot above the bag.

On double steals it is necessary to throw a little higher, so
that if a cutoff is indicated the fielder making the cutoff can
take the ball about shoulder-high, which leaves him in perfect
throwing position to return the ball to the plate, or else can
let the ball go through if the runner on third doesn't break for
the plate.

Frequently the catcher can assist in breaking up a double steal
by bluffing the throw to second and wheeling to throw to
third. Or he can reverse this by looking toward third to drive
that runner back and then throwing through to second. It is a
strange psychological fact that catchers can bluff runners back
to third merely by facing in that direction, without making the
bluff throw.

Zach Taylor, who was named to manage the Browns for
1948, saw a lot of service as a catcher in both National and
American Leagues and he was much impressed with the psychological factors which enter into double steals. When he was
with the Giants in 1927, he nailed Leslie Mann of the Braves

on a double steal twice in the same game and in the same manner.

"The Braves had a man on first and third and Mr. McGraw signaled from the bench that if they attempted a double steal I was to bluff the throw to second and then throw to third, when Mann was the base runner," Taylor relates. "I did as I was instructed and was able to pick Leslie off third.

"Four or five innings later, the same play came up and McGraw gave me the same sign. I was surprised because I knew that Mann was a smart ballplayer and I wondered how Mac expected him to fall for the same play twice. I went through with it and again picked Mann off. Then I realized that the Old Man had been thinking along with Leslie. He knew that Leslie wouldn't expect us to catch him the same way twice and that therefore I would throw through to second this time. McGraw simply thought right along with Mann and outguessed him because he knew what Leslie was thinking."

A catcher can help himself by bluff throws to keep runners close to the base. Sometimes he can pick a runner off first when a bunt or a hit-and-run has been prevented by a pitch-out and sometimes, but far less frequently, he can pick a runner off third when a squeeze play goes sour. Throwing to second to pick a runner off is risky business and should be attempted only on a set play, such as the Cardinals pulled against us in the 1943 World Series.

On the subject of set plays to pick runners off second, the Dodgers used one back in 1920, a year in which they won the pennant. Taylor, who was a member of that club, told me about it. I have never seen it attempted except by kid and sandlot teams, yet strangely enough it was worked occasionally by Brooklyn.

In this play the second baseman and shortstop kept their normal positions, leaving the runner on second free to take an exceptionally long lead. Then Hy Myers, the Brooklyn center fielder, who played shallow most of the time anyway, would charge in from the outfield to take a quick throw from the catcher at second.

Zach Taylor is the authority for this story when he was with the Dodgers: playing an extra-inning game against the Cubs in Chicago, the Dodgers attempted the set play when the Cubs had a man on second with two out.

"Rowdy Elliott was catching for us, and I was on the bench when the play was signaled," Taylor says. "Myers came charging in, and Rowdy made a bad throw, the ball going about 5 feet over Myers's head. That was the end of the game, of course; but there was a screwy turn—as there always was when the Dodgers were involved in anything. Playing right field for us was Tommy Griffith, a hustling ballplayer of the Pepper Martin type. He raced over to back up Myers and hounded the ball until he got it in the deepest part of center field. Then he whirled to throw the ball back to the infield and discovered that he was the only ballplayer of either team still on the field!"

Some catchers hamper pitchers with a man on base by concentrating on the runner instead of the batter, precisely as some pitchers hamper themselves under similar conditions. The catcher should always realize that his prime duty is to assist the pitcher in retiring the batter. That comes first. The catcher should prevent the steal entirely on his own.

Therefore a catcher should not be too anxious to call for pitch-outs unless he is almost certain that a steal, a bunt, or a hit-and-run will be attempted. To call for a pitch-out merely as protection against a stolen base is to give the batter a big edge on the pitcher, since it helps to put the count in the batter's favor.

There are also catchers who show a tendency to signal for fast balls with a man on, because fast balls are easier to handle.

Batters take full advantage of catchers who have reputations for being afraid to call for a curve, a change of pace, a knuckler, etc., with a runner on first. They know that they're almost certain to get a fast ball and they make their plans accordingly.

When Dutch Leonard was with Washington he said that the addition of Rick Ferrell to the team helped him immensely. Ferrell was one catcher who wasn't afraid to call for Dutch's knuckler in a pinch, and Leonard could use his most effective pitch at the time he needed it most, instead of having to rely on a fast ball, with the batter knowing in advance that in all probability he would get a fast one.

Another of the catcher's duties is to field bunts in front of the plate, and here his agility can be a great help to the club. A catcher who pounces on a bunted ball can frequently turn the bunt into a double play. Although it seems a simple thing to pick up a bunt barehanded and make the play, two hands are recommended, with the mitt being put in front of the ball to block its progress. This is because bunted balls usually have plenty of "English," or backspin, and take strange hops away from the catcher if he hasn't his mitt on the ground to assist in fielding the ball. Like the third baseman on swinging bunts, the catcher should never take his eye off the ball until he has picked it up. Nor should he ever throw the ball before he has fielded it. That's rule number one.

On bunted balls which are handled by the pitcher, the catcher should hustle down and cover third, in the event that the runner on first, who has been bunted to second, has his head up and makes for the unprotected base. On all infield plays, except when a man is on third, the catcher should back up the first baseman to protect against an overthrow. The third baseman or pitcher will cover the plate under these conditions.

When there is a play to the plate, the catcher should get on the third-base side of the plate and brace himself firmly for the crash of the runner. With all his armor, there is no excuse for a catcher's letting a runner upset him or get by him. The ball should be held in the glove, protected by the "meat hand," and the glove held in front of the plate so the runner must slide into the ball. If the throw arrives so far in advance of the runner that he checks himself and attempts to return to third, the catcher should chase the runner back toward third and throw immediately to the third baseman in order to get the run-down started as quickly as possible.

The catcher's most complicated job is calling the pitches by signs. The general pattern of signs which the catcher gives with the fingers of his bare hand is the same in the major leagues as it is on the sand lots: one finger for a fast one, two for a curve, three for a slow-up or change of pace, and wiggling fingers for a pitch-out. Sometimes a clenched fist is used for the pitch-out. Some of the catchers who play rough throw a handful of dust or jerk a thumb upward for a "duster." We'll go into no signs for dusters or bean-balls here.

Earlier in this chapter it was explained how the catcher gives the signs and the protection he uses to hide these signs from the coaches and base runners. There is a variation of this in which the catcher gives a combination of signals, such as two fingers, one finger, two fingers, having previously established which of the three signs is the real one.

Sometimes a catcher will have a signal which indicates which of the combination signs is the McCoy. For example, he may wipe his bare hand across his chest protector to indicate that the first of the multiple signs is the one which counts, or rest his gloved hand on his left knee to indicate that it is the second sign from which the pitcher must take his cue.

Whatever this prearranged signal may be, it must be a natural gesture so the offensive team will not be tipped off. Either of the gestures mentioned here would be natural mannerisms of any catcher. And there are many others, such as adjusting the mask with a pat of the bare hand.

It is one of the strange things in baseball that despite all the complex systems of signs invented, the basic pattern remains the same: one for a fast one, two for a curve. So deeply rooted in the game is this system that "number two" is accepted baseball talk for a curve ball the country over.

Because the runner on second is in an excellent position to spot the catcher's signs, it is a common practice to use an entirely different set of signals in that situation. If the multiple-sign system is being used, the first sign may be the true one with a runner on second, the second sign the true one under all other conditions.

When the runner does steal a sign and relay it to the batter, however, the batter keeps a poker face when he receives the information. Billy Herman, who managed Pittsburgh in 1947, was especially good at stealing signs from second base and was a big help to the Dodgers when he joined them in 1941. Dixie Walker reciprocated one day in an important game against the Cardinals when he was on second and Herman at bat.

"I caught the sign that Mort Cooper was going to throw a curve and relayed the information to Billy," said Dixie. "His eyes opened so wide I thought sure Cooper would get wise, because I could notice them from second base. But Mort didn't, and Billy hit the curve for two bases to score me with the only run of the game."

Joe McCarthy has a favorite story about stealing signs from second base. It happened in 1926, his first year with the Cubs.

"It was our first series in Brooklyn, and I held a meeting of the Cubs before the game," Joe tells it. "I was going over the Dodger hitters, asking the Cub players for information, when one of our veteran pitchers came into the meeting late and somewhat the worse for wear. It was my first year and this fellow had been a big star, so I didn't say anything until he found himself a seat in the back of the room, where he promptly went to sleep.

"There were a couple of grins from the players, but I knew this wasn't the time or the place for discipline so I ignored the whole thing and went right on with the meeting.

"Rabbit Maranville, who had been with the Cubs the year before, was now with Brooklyn, so I cautioned the players about Rab. I said that once he got to second base, he'd get every sign on our club if we weren't extra careful.

"Just then this pitcher in the back of the room came to, sat up and said, 'I wouldn't worry about Rab, Joe. Let me pitch and he won't get to second base all day.'

"That broke up the meeting."

10: Playing the Outfield

"OUTFIELDERS SHOULD pay their way into the park."

This, of course, is baseball's saddest gag.

As an outfielder, I'm not going to defend our right to free admission or claim that we're as busy as a catcher. The statistics show that outfielders average about three chances a game, which is slightly less than the third baseman's daily work. In some games the fans see an outfielder stand around for so many innings with nothing to do that they wonder why he doesn't take a chair out to his position with him.

The fact is that an outfielder who does a real job for his club works as hard as anyone in baseball. He covers a position as extensive as an oversized building lot, a position to which every fly ball hit will drop either as a safe hit or a put-out. In the outfield there is no such thing as a muff and a recovery in time to make the put-out, except in the rare instance of the deliberate trapping of a fly ball to make a force play on a runner already on base.

A muff in the outfield usually is worse even than an infielder's error on a sure double-play ball. A missed ball not only breaks the pitcher's heart because it robs him of an out which he has earned, but frequently goes for extra bases and allows a run or more to score.

And by "muff" I don't mean only the actual mishandling of a ball. An outfielder may play a ball in absolutely errorless fashion, so far as the box score is concerned, but still be guilty of a tremendous flop if he fails to get the jump on a ball that he might have caught and lets it fall safe. A team is far better off with an outfielder who piles up errors trying for hard catches than with one who handles perfectly every ball hit to him but doesn't go after the tough ones.

In addition to his fielding skill, an outfielder must carry his share, or more than his share, of the wood to the plate. An outfielder who can't hit around .300 should be a Tris Speaker or a Terry Moore defensively if he isn't to be a drag on the club. And the days of the outfielder who's a good hitter but a poor fielder are gone, probably forever.

There used to be outfielders who were heavy hitters but clumsy fielders, fellows who would knock in two runs but kick away three; but you don't see them around any more. To be an outfielder in the majors today a player must be a good, consistent hitter, exceptionally fast if he isn't a long-ball hitter, and a first-rate fly-chaser and thrower. Otherwise he won't be up very long.

The lively ball and the bigger parks have put bigger chores on the outfielders. Since the early 1920's they have had to play deeper and go back farther. And because they have to play deeper, they have to cover far more ground between their normal positions and the infield.

Although he may not handle the ball for innings at a stretch, the outfielder must be on his toes for every play. Because he now plays deep, a runner is much more likely to try to go from first to third on an outfield single, and the fielder must be adept at handling ground balls and throwing to keep the runner from taking the extra base.

Before every play an outfielder must size up all the possibilities. He must know the hitter. He must know the ground conditions—whether the bounce is likely to be hard or soft. He must know what the wind currents will do to a fly ball, how backgrounds, shadows, or haze will distort his vision, how he will play the ball if it is beyond him and against the fence.

The outfielder must try to make every catch in the best possible position from which to throw. Some players like to catch the ball in front of them, with hands outstretched. My own preference is to take fly balls with my hands above my head, with my left foot toward the plate. I've found that from that position I can save time making the throw.

On ground balls an outfielder rarely has any choice; when he catches up with it the ball usually will be hugging the ground. But if it happens to be a bounding ball, he should charge it in order to field it at the top of the hop, leaving him in good throwing position.

In the 1942 World Series, Enos Slaughter, playing right field for the Cardinals, saved the second game for his club when he caught a bounding ball shoulder-high and threw out the Yankees' potential tying run trying to go from first to third on a single in the ninth. Had he fielded the ball at his feet he would never have been able to straighten up and make the throw in time to get the runner.

Pregame fielding practice ought to give the outfielder a fairly accurate idea of ground conditions. If the ground is soft from recent rains, the ball will hug the grass. If the ground is hard, the ball will take hard, fast hops.

If the outfield is bumpy, and sometimes it is, even in big-league parks, the outfielder must try to get in front of the ball to block it with his body if it takes a bad hop. The sight of a ground ball getting away from an outfielder and going for extra bases is extremely painful to the pitcher and everyone else except the batting team and their fans.

In the big parks the wind can be very tricky, shifting from inning to inning, and the fielder should take an occasional look at the flags around the stands to learn which way it's blowing.

The effects of backgrounds and shadows must be learned by experience. Observations during pregame practice aren't of much help, since the conditions change as the sun sets. And crowded stands, with thousands of fans smoking, make game conditions far different from those in the practice period. Before the game the crowd is small, and haze from tobacco smoke is at a minimum. As the game goes on the haze deepens, especially if the day is humid and there is no breeze to carry the smoke from the park.

Backgrounds vary with the seasons. In Yankee Stadium, for instance, the haze is a greater problem in the fall than in spring and summer. Even with sunglasses an outfielder is likely to become confused. My own dodge is to shield my eyes with my hand as the pitch is being delivered. I find that it gives me a better perspective and makes it easier to follow the delivery to the bat.

Because conditions vary not only with the seasons but in every ball park and with the position of the sun, the knack of finding the ball against tricky backgrounds must be cultivated through experience and observation. Eventually the fielder will find himself perfectly at home in his own park regardless of the variations.

Playing a ball as it caroms off a fence is another problem that varies according to ball parks and must also be solved by experience. Naturally, the sharper the angle of the ball's path to the fence the wider the bounce should be back onto the field. Mel Ott, in the Polo Grounds, Tommy Henrich, in Yankee Stadium, and Dixie Walker, in Ebbets Field, are three outfielders who had this play down to an exact science in their own parks.

The most important thing about outfielding is getting a jump on the ball. The most common excuse of an outfielder who just does not get up to a fly ball is, "I didn't get a jump on it." The most usual explanation of an exceptional outfield catch is, "I got a good jump on it."

Getting the jump is merely making a quick start after a fly ball, and the outfielder roaming a wide expanse of ball park to pull down a real blast that seemed sure for extra bases is a sight which thrills fans and fills them with wonder at the outfielder's intuitive powers.

After more than ten years a friend of mine still talks about the day he saw Earl Combs, the old Yankee center fielder, make nine put-outs in one game.

"It seemed that every time the pitcher started his delivery Combs started to move," he says. "One ball he'd catch way over in right field and the very next one deep in left. It didn't look as if he was running very fast, but he was always there waiting for the ball. It looked like black magic, the way he knew just where to be."

Combs was a wonderful fly-catcher. He didn't need black magic to put him under the ball as it descended. He simply knew how to get the jump on it.

A prime necessity in getting the jump on the ball is knowing the hitter, knowing where he is likely to hit certain types of pitches. For instance, ballplayers know that my power is to left, that if I hit an inside curve I am likely to pull it down the left-field foul line, that if I connect with an outside curve it will probably go just to right of center. They know that Johnny Mize pulls inside pitches down the right-field line.

Most major-league fans have seen Connie Mack standing on the step of the Athletics' dugout waving his score card, motioning to an outfielder to go over a few steps. He was communicating to the outfielder his knowledge of the hitter.

As the pitcher prepares to deliver the ball the outfielder is up on his toes, moving forward, ready to move in any direction the instant the ball is hit. The phrase "off with the crack of the bat," while romantic, is really meaningless, since the outfielder should be in motion long before he hears the sound of the ball meeting the bat. Through experience and practice the outfielder acquires a working knowledge of the probable distance and speed of the hit from the first quick glance he gets at it as it begins its flight.

The sooner the outfielder gets to the spot where the ball is descending the more easily he can make the catch. There are many times, of course, when the fielder must make the catch on the dead run; but when he is standing still it is easier and surer. When there is a runner on third who could score after the catch, the outfielder, after getting the jump on the fly, may slow down in order to take the ball deliberately on the run to increase the force of his throw to the plate.

No outfielder is a real workman unless he can turn his back on the ball, run his legs off, and take the catch over his shoulder. Outfielders should practice this play until they are sure of it. Backpedaling outfielders get nowhere on balls hit behind them. On many such balls the fielder may be able to turn after his run and make the catch facing the infield, but frequently there is no time to turn.

For the fan the diving, or shoestring, catch is one of the most spectacular plays in the outfielder's repertoire. For the player, for his team, it is one of the most speculative. Since it deprives the batter of a sure base hit, it gives a real lift to the pitcher; but it is not routine play.

There are times when it should be attempted, and times when it is far better to play it safe and field the ball on the hop. That means giving the batter a single; but a miss on an attempted diving catch gives him a three-bagger, or maybe a home run if the park is big enough.

The diving catch is a play on which the outfielder has to make his decision in a split second. He must have weighed all the possibilities beforehand—the score, the inning, the men on base. Unless the outfielder is really skillful at this type of catch, he should never gamble on making it unless the conditions are such that a base hit means the ball game to his club. If there are two out, and such a catch means cutting off a run, he is justified in the gamble only if the run is an important one, such as the winning or tying run. If his club is ahead, he should never attempt the catch if a miss would permit the tying runs to move into scoring position.

There is a story about Yankees' diving catches in the last ball game Babe Ruth ever pitched. It was the last day of the season, and he defeated the Red Sox in Boston. They scored three runs on him because of a timely triple to left-center. Dusty Cooke, later a trainer for the Philadelphia Phillies, played center for the Yankees that day. The triple, a low line drive, was hit between Cooke and the left fielder, and Dusty had to come across the path of the ball on a straight line to catch it. He just missed connections.

On the way back to New York, Ruth was kidding Cooke about the ball's getting away from him.

"You know, Dusty," said Babe, "I'd have had a shutout if you'd dived for that ball."

"Well, Babe, I'll tell you," Cooke replied. "I was debating diving for that ball."

Since Cooke had all of four-fifths of a second to make up his mind, it must have been the shortest debate on record.

The rule about catching a ball with two hands rather than one whenever possible applies to outfielders as well as infielders. There will be times, however, when an outfielder must take a fly one-handed because he can't reach the ball with both hands. An outfielder can reach as much as 2 feet farther for a ball with his gloved hand than he can when trying to make the catch with both hands.

It does an outfielder no harm to take an occasional infield workout, since this will sharpen his judgment and his handling of ground balls. Even in the fielding of ground balls, the "jump" is important to an outfielder, because it enables him to field the ball directly in front of him and lessens the chances that it will go through him.

Balls which a right-hander hits to right or right-center have a tendency to slice toward the foul line, and balls to left and left-center tend to hook toward the left-field foul line. Outfield hits by a left-hander act just the reverse. There isn't much slice or hook to balls hit directly to center, but the center fielder must make allowances for slices and hooks on balls hit to either side of him.

The better the right and left fielders can protect the foul lines the stronger the team's defense. In parks with short foul lines this isn't so important, but in larger parks a ball which is hit down the foul line and which isn't fielded always spells extra bases. Experience will teach right and left fielders just how far in they can play and still cover balls hit between themselves and the foul line.

In playing the hitter, the outfielder should insist on getting the signs from the shortstop so that he will know in which direction to break. Curve balls are more likely to be pulled than fast balls. An outfielder should watch how the infielders are playing a hitter and govern himself accordingly.

With a man on base, the outfielder must have his mind made up in advance on where he will throw, but he should react instantly to any change in circumstances. The safest rule to follow is: always throw ahead of the runner. Suppose, for instance, there is a man on second, and the outfielder, who is set for a throw to the plate in the event a single is hit to his territory, fumbles the ball. Now he must decide whether he has any chance to catch the runner with a throw to the plate or whether he should throw to second to prevent the batter from moving into scoring position on a useless throw home.

An outfielder's throws must always be governed by the score. If his team has a two-run lead, it is far more important for him to keep the tying run from reaching second base, and thus getting into scoring position, than it is for him to attempt to throw a runner out at the plate. He may miss the play at the plate, and the important tying run will be allowed to advance an extra base on the throw.

On throws to all bases, including home, a throw on one hop is preferable to a throw on the fly. A bounding throw is more accurate and far easier for the infielder to handle, particularly if a situation develops which gives him an opportunity to make a cutoff play. And bounce throws are far less likely to get away from the man making the catch.

I can always remember a throw I made in my first year with the Yankees, a throw which was spectacular and pleased the fans but left my manager, Joe McCarthy, unimpressed.

It was in the ninth inning of a September game against Detroit. The Tigers had men on first and third in the ninth with one out, and we had a 6 to 5 lead. Charley Gehringer was the hitter and he drove a long fly to me. I cut loose with the peg home to stop Pete Fox from scoring with the tying run. The ball carried all the way to Bill Dickey on a line, and he tagged Fox to end the game. I got a terrific hand from the stands; when I reached the clubhouse all I got from McCarthy was a look.

"What are you trying to do, Joe?" he asked quietly. "Show me how strong you are?"

There was no use in telling him that I had honestly intended to get the ball to Dickey on the bounce but had miscalculated the distance. It would have sounded like an alibi, and no manager wants to hear alibis.

A story which Al Moore tells about just such a throw makes me know how lightly I got off. Moore played the outfield with the Cardinals and the Giants. One day when he was a rookie with the Giants he was sent to left field to replace Irish Meusel, a fine hitter but a weak thrower. A runner was on second. The batter singled to left. Moore threw all the way to the plate on the fly, nailing the runner and ending the inning.

Moore trotted happily to the bench, expecting to hear words of praise from Manager McGraw. What he heard was this: "Moore, I thought I explained to you that I always wanted throws from the outfield to take one hop, in case a cutoff is necessary. You probably think you've made a fine throw. You've heard those fans cheering you and you think you're big stuff. I'll show you how big you are in relation to the team.

"Suppose I put a sign up which says, 'Tomorrow afternoon there will be a throwing exhibition by Al Moore at the Polo Grounds.' How many fans do you think it would attract? You wouldn't get fifty. I could and should fine you fifty, but I won't. In the future, just remember that the fans came here to see the Giants play, not to see Al Moore exercise his arm."

There is, however, an exception to the bounce-throw rule when the field is soft as the result of overnight rains or a drizzle during the game. Then, if the outfielder is close enough to reach his base without a bounce, he would throw the ball all the way. If a ball hits a soft spot on a wet field it doesn't "take off," it merely dribbles toward the target.

On a relay the outfielder should remember that his throw, the first throw, must be the long one. An infielder who goes out to take a relay should not roam so far that his throw is a long one, unless, of course, he has a weak-throwing outfielder, and there aren't many of those in the big leagues.

Ever since Tris Speaker played for the Red Sox and Cleveland—and Tris started his career before I was born—there has been a red-hot debate about the advantages and disadvantages of an outfielder's playing short, or "shallow," as the ballplayers call it. I don't think it is possible to play a shallow outfield in these days of the lively ball.

An outfielder who can play short is invaluable to his ball

club. He can catch many damaging Texas-league flies which ordinarily would fall for singles. In fact, Speaker, twice in one season, made unassisted double plays at second base because of his ability to catch these bloopers just over the infield.

The hardest thing for an outfielder to do is to go back on a fly ball. Apparently Speaker could do this better than anybody else, and because of this rare ability he could afford to play shallow. But Speaker was a genius, at least one of the greatest outfielders who ever lived. I advise the average outfielder to play deep, rather than shallow, because it is comparatively easy for him to come in for a fly ball. An occasional ball which might drop between an outfielder and the infield can't cause nearly as much harm as a ball hit over his head which he could have caught if he had been playing normally deep.

There are times when an outfielder must play shallow. Such a time is when his team is in the field in the last half of the ninth inning, and the other club has the winning run on third and less than two out. In such a setup, a long fly ball wins the game anyway, so it doesn't matter whether the outfielder catches it or not. And by playing shallow he has a chance to catch a Texas-league single and an even chance to throw out the runner on any fly ball he catches. This is an exception, a case which won't come up more than two or three times in any one season.

All outfielders should wear sunglasses. This may sound like gratuitous advice in this era of night games, but baseball has to come into the sunshine occasionally, and then the fielder, even if not playing the sun field, must have his glasses.

The sun field is so tough to play that it requires almost a special instinct in an outfielder. There will be occasions when every outfielder has to take a ball against the sun, but this is a handicap under which the sun-fielder works all the time. The only suggestion for sun-fielders is to try to gauge the ball by getting a sidewise glimpse and shielding his eyes with his glove.

Never look directly into the sun. Even with sunglasses, no fielder can take a ball coming out of the sun.

Outfielders should always be quick to back up defensive plays, in the infield as well as in the outfield. The center fielder should be moving forward on all plays at second base, the right fielder on plays to first base, and the left fielder on plays to third. The center fielder comes directly in to protect overthrows or other errors at second base, but the left and right fielders should, in most cases, advance at an angle to the foul line. This is because an overthrow of those bases is likely to hit the stands and carom off.

It is, of course, essential for outfielders to back each other up whenever possible. Sometimes even the most experienced of outfielders will "lose" a ball for any of a number of reasons, and the other fielder, if he is alert, can make the saving catch. And, of course, an extra base can be prevented when one outfielder backs up another on base hits.

Outfielders should remember at all times when they are chasing a fly ball that another outfielder, and sometimes an infielder, may be chasing the same ball. All three will be running with their heads back, watching only the ball. The only way to avoid a collision is for the outfielder to yell that he has the ball under control, and to keep his ears open for the shouts of the other players.

Once the outfielder hears another player calling "I have it!" he should immediately take his eyes off the ball and locate the other player. Sometimes it will be necessary for one outfielder to throw himself to the ground to avoid a crash. Whatever the way out, take it; for a collision means not only that one or more players may be injured, but that the fly ball won't be caught at all.

On fly balls hit between infield and outfield (Texas leaguers) the outfielder should call for the ball and make the catch whenever he can reach it, for he has the play in front of him and will be in a better throwing position. On balls to the outfield, the outfielder who can make the catch in the best throwing position should get the right of way.

Some outfielders, notably Tommy Henrich of the Yanks, are particularly good at coming in for short flies and, with a man on first, trapping the ball and getting a force-out at second. This is a dangerous play and should be attempted only by the experts. In the first place, the chances of a double play on such a trap are almost nonexistent, unless the batter fails to run out his hit; and the only advantage, a slight one, is that the fielder may force a fast runner at second, leaving a slow runner on first.

Henrich could confuse the opposition with runners on first and second because of his adroitness at trapping the ball. When he first bluffed a catch and then trapped the ball under these conditions, he usually had both runners moving in opposite directions. I repeat, however, this is no maneuver for the novice. I once saw one of our Yankee outfielders, not Tommy, attempt this play and he wound up throwing the ball into the Red Sox dugout at Fenway Park.

There are times, of course, when the skillful outfielder can bluff the runner on first so that he comes too far down, in which case the outfielder can catch the fly and double him at first. Plays like this, however, demand perfect coordination and a world of experience.

One simple defense play which the outfielder should perfect is the bluff catch on Texas leaguers. This is simply charging the ball with arms outstretched, giving the impression that it can be caught. This naturally causes the base runners to hold up and often paves the way for a force-out. At least it prevents the runner from taking too long a lead and thus getting an extra base on the Texas leaguer.

On all flies which the outfielder catches near the infield, flies so short that a runner couldn't possibly score from third after the catch, the fielder should get the ball back to the infield as quickly as possible, without resorting to bluff throws. On flies of this type, the runner on third will make a bluff run to the plate to draw a throw, in the hope that the outfielder will throw hurriedly and wildly. Under these circumstances, the smartest thing for the outfielder to do is get the ball to the nearest infielder, thus throttling any sneak run for the plate and eliminating entirely the possibility of a bad throw from the greater distance.

There is one outfielding assignment that no baseball guide-book describes. That's the detail of playing straight man to the patter of the fans. It's part of the job. The outfielders, especially the right and left fielders, are the players whose positions bring them nearest to the stands and place them most readily in range of the yelling of the fans.

The people in the stands are as much a part of professional baseball as the players on the field. Sometimes they sandpaper an outfielder down to a thin finish. No man in his right mind enjoys being called "bum," "punk," "palooka," or worse, or having his personal affairs described to a park full of people by a voice that could call close-order drill for a whole army corps. But any man who plays professional baseball must be as ready to accept a going over as he is to receive a burst of applause for a nice catch or a timely hit.

Just as the player's tools are his bat and glove, the fan's equipment is his lungs, and the fan has as much right to holler as a player has to take his turn at bat or to jockey an opponent. Moreover, the crowd noise usually balances itself—a good play will bring as much appreciation as a boner brings abuse.

No matter how partial a crowd may be to its home team, it usually gives the visitor a sporting break and polices itself to see that its sportsmanship is not violated. Mel Ott tells a perfect story of this.

It was a Sunday game in St. Louis, in the middle of a pennant fight between the Giants and the Cards, with Carl Hubbell and Dizzy Dean pitching before an overflow crowd parked behind ropes all around the outfield.

"The fans were on me all day, principally because Hub was outpitching Diz, and also because I was the nearest Giant player to them," Mel tells it. "Hub was really great, on a day when almost any ordinary fly would fall into the crowd for a ground-rule double.

"The Cards not only didn't get a ground-rule double, but not one of them hit a fly to our outfielders until about the sixth, when I caught a soft fly in right. Just as I caught this ball I was hit in the middle of the back with a pop bottle.

"I got rid of the ball and looked around, and there was almost a riot among the fans parked behind me. They found the guy who threw the bottle and worked him over, and for the rest of the game everything they yelled at me was friendly and encouraging."

Jockeys in the stands are like jockeys on the bench. Some of them are sharp, and some just noisy. Some can make a point out of any situation. Old-timers still tell of a crack that was made when the late Fatty Fothergill, a hard-hitting American League outfielder, knocked himself out in a White Sox exhibition game in Roanoke, Virginia, when he chased a fly ball and crashed into the fence. The crash splintered the fence.

An announcer (this was before the days of the public address system) rushed onto the field with a megaphone and shouted, "Is there a doctor in the stands?"

From right above the spot where Fothergill had fallen, a fan yelled back, "Is there a carpenter in the stands?"

From the next section came another call: "Is there an out-fielder in the stands?"

11: Hitting

A GAME OF baseball, sifted down to rock bottom, is a duel between the batter and the pitcher. Almost every play (pick-offs and hidden-ball tricks excepted) starts with the delivery of the ball to the plate. The batter's teammates are on deck to move him around the bases and make him score; the pitcher's are in the field to help him prevent the score.

The batter and the pitcher stand 60 feet 6 inches apart, the distance from mound to plate. The pitcher is posted on a mound 15 inches high at its highest point. The batter stands in a space 4 feet wide and 6 feet long—the box.

The pitcher's ammunition is a tightly sewn, leather-covered ball not quite 3 inches in diameter and weighing about 5 ounces. Sometimes to the batter it looks as small and as active as a Mexican jumping bean.

The batter's weapon is a wooden club no more than 42 inches long, 2¾ inches thick at its fattest part, weighing a little more than 2 pounds and usually made of ash. Pitchers occasionally think it's as big as the whole tree.

The pitcher shoots the ball to the plate at a speed of almost 100 miles per hour,* and with tricks. By finger grips and wrist twists he can make it curve to left or right, or slide, glide, or hop. But to have it count as a strike he must get it over some portion of the 12-inch width of the plate and somewhere between the batter's shoulders and knees.

The batter's mission is to drive the ball beyond or safely

---

* In 1946, a United States Army timing device clocked Bob Feller's fast ball at 146 feet per second at the regulation pitching distance of 60 feet 6 inches—a speed of 99.5 miles per hour.

among the nine agile, glue-fingered members of the defensive team. He has the time between the ball's departure from the pitcher's fingers and its arrival at the plate in which to decide whether it is a good one or a bad one, whether to take it or let it go by, and (if he decides to swing) to get the bat around and connect. This time is two-fifths of a second.

Since the decision must be made and the action taken in a period of time scarcely long enough to strike a match, let alone a streak of ball, a player who is a good, consistent hitter has to be blessed with a fortunate stock of physical and mental attributes.

He has to have a sharp eye, quick reflexes, good timing, judgment, confidence, and strength of arms, wrists, and shoulders. Baseball people say that the good hitter is born, not made. They mean that he is the fellow who was lucky enough to be born with those attributes.

They do not mean that some people are born as .330 hitters and others as .220 hitters, but merely that some have greater natural gifts than others for connecting a baseball bat solidly with a pitched ball. All, however, have to make the most of what they have by practice—developing a sound, smooth swing, correcting faults, studying the pitcher to know (in advance if possible) what kind of ball he is about to throw.

On my list, keen vision is the first requirement for good hitting. If you can't see it you can't hit it. This vision necessary for good hitting is what the doctors call good stereoscopic vision: perception of depth and an ability to judge position in space. Without it the air cadet with 20-20 vision in each eye washes out of pilot training. If he can't sense the depth of his plane in relation to the ground, he is unable to land it. More familiarly, the automobile driver who can't judge correctly the distance of his right front fender from other objects on his right lacks depth perception.

Provided he has the other attributes, a player who wears glasses to correct his vision may be a good hitter. My brother Dom is a good example of a consistent hitter who wears glasses. And Paul Waner, one of the steadiest hitters in baseball, was using glasses when he made his 3,000th hit. He is one of the very few batters to reach that total.

However good vision is obtained, no one ever became a real hitter without it. When John Kieran, the "Information Please" talking encyclopedia who used to be a sports writer, was asked what made Babe Ruth such a great home-run hitter, he replied instantly, "His eyes," and told several stories to demonstrate the Babe's keen eyesight.

When they went duck hunting Babe would spot the birds long before they were visible to anyone else in the blind, including the guide. Kieran used to test Ruth's vision by getting him to read the license number of an automobile so far away that he himself couldn't even tell the color of the plate.

Ted Williams, certainly one of the greatest hitters in the game, has wonderful eyesight. When he was in naval aviation during the war he broke many records in vision tests used to examine air cadets. Rogers Hornsby, one of the best hitters of all time, regarded vision as so important to his batting that in the more than twenty years of his active major-league career he never once went to a movie; he wanted to avoid every use of his eyes that was not absolutely necessary.

Whatever his natural attributes may be, there are two elements of hitting over which the batter can have full control—the type of bat he uses, and how he swings it.

There are bats of many sizes and weights, and the player should experiment until he finds the one which he can swing most comfortably. There are long bats and short ones, heavy ones and light ones, thin- and thick-handled bats. A good rule to follow in choosing a bat is to take the heaviest one which can be swung without difficulty. In spring training I always use a heavy bat, then switch to a lighter one for the season. Hitting practice will show the player which type of bat has the proper balance for his individual needs.

The batter's box is a space 4 feet wide and 6 feet long, the short side toward the pitcher, the inside line being 4 inches from the plate. A box is lined off on each side of the plate, one for right-handed hitters, one for left-handers. All hitting must be done from within the box.

In discussing the swing, let's illustrate with a right-hander. The first consideration is the stance, the position of the batter's feet as he addresses the plate. There are three stances: the even stance, in which both feet are the same distance from the inside line of the box; the closed stance, in which the left foot is closer to the inside line; and the open stance, in which the right foot is closer to the inside line.

The main thing about the stance is that it must be comfortable. Every player, whether he hits .220 or .400, has a stance that is naturally more comfortable than any other position. If he feels in any way awkward or "tied up," it will affect his stride, his timing, and his swing.

Once the pitcher takes his position on the mound preparatory to delivering the ball to the plate, the batter must be ready to hit and must follow the ball every second. He must never take his eyes off the ball from the time the pitcher begins his motion until the ball has been hit or has plopped into the catcher's mitt.

Some hitters stand far back in the batter's box, some closer to the forward line. Most batters grip the bat with the two hands close together (although Ty Cobb and Honus Wagner, two of the greatest hitters the game ever knew, held their hands a few inches apart as they addressed the plate, sliding them together as they swung). Almost all batters use a plain grip, the fingers of each hand flat against the handle (although Ernie Lombardi used an interlocking grip, with the little finger of his right hand laced between the forefinger and second finger of his left). Frank Frisch came up to the majors from Fordham University batting cross-handed, placing the hand nearer the pitcher above the other hand on the bat, but he dropped that style after a year.

Most long-ball hitters hold the bat at the extreme end, many enclosing the knob in the palm of the bottom hand. My grip is at the extreme end, with just the knob showing. Choke hitters grip the bat at least 4 inches from the end. Whatever the grip and the stance, they must put the fat part of the bat over the heart of the plate.

Batters who take preliminary waggles with the bat frequently find themselves out of position when the ball is delivered. The less bat-waving a hitter does, the better set he is when the ball is delivered.

The batter stands up at the plate with his weight on his right foot (remember we're illustrating with a right-hander), spikes gripping the ground firmly, knees slightly relaxed to give them flexibility, bat held in a comfortable position off the right shoulder.

Now for the swing itself. The swing must be level—the bat traveling in a plane parallel to the ground. No batter can get all his power into a swing that is not level. Batters who swing down on the ball merely beat it into the dirt for easily handled grounders, which often result in double plays. Batters who swing up on the ball raise easy flies. As Jimmy Dykes, then managing the White Sox, said to a pinch hitter who had lifted a high pop foul to the catcher, "You gave an excellent imitation of a man hitting out of a well."

Don't be an uppercutter or a wood chopper. While no batter can select his brand of eyesight, his reflexes, or his muscles, every batter can cultivate a level swing. Keeping the left elbow

THE SWING'S THE THING!

◄ Detroit outfielder Ty Cobb (1886–1961), one of the greatest base runners in the history of the game, touching third base without interrupting his stride. Circa 1915. HULTON ARCHIVE/ GETTY IMAGES

troit Tigers outfielder Ty Cobb sliding safely. Circa 1925.
LTON ARCHIVE/ GETTY IMAGES

▲ The Mighty Bambino in Action. An International Action-graph of Babe Ruth, mighty slugger of the American League champion Yankees, completing the swing that resulted in so many home runs. The three photos on the left picture the motions of the swing; the three on the right show the powerful follow-through employed by the Bambino. Photographed June 7, 1922. © BETTMANN/CORBIS

▲ A rare shot of Babe Ruth sliding safely in a Yankee–Detroit Tiger game in August 1934. The catcher is Ray Hayworth. Usually, the Babe tiptoed across home plate in a more placid fashion. AP PHOTO

◀ George Herman (Babe) Ruth, former Yankee outfielder and champion home-run hitter of all time. His eyes were so keen that he could read the license numbers of an automobile when others could not even make out the colors of the plate. WILLIAM C. GREENE, WORLD-TELEGRAM

▲ Joe DiMaggio, as outfielder for the San Francisco Seals, July 26, 1935. The ne
season he was called up to the majors as a member of the New York Yankees.
was as favorably known for his powerful throws to home plate as he was for h
hitting. AP Photo

DiMaggio knocks one of Cliff Melton's left-handed offerings out of the park in the fifth game of the 1937 Yankee–Giant World Series. Note the complete follow-through of the swing. WILLIAM C. GREENE, WORLD-TELEGRAM

Joe DiMaggio goes to bat in the fourth inning of the game with the St. Louis Browns in Yankee Stadium (June 26, 1941) in an attempt to keep up his consecutive game hitting streak. Although not succeeding this time at bat, DiMaggio hit a double in the first inning to stretch the streak to 38 consecutive games. The Yankees won, 4 to 1. © BETTMANN/CORBIS

MELTON

DIMAGGIO

DANNING

ORMSBY

▲ Joe DiMaggio, New York Yankees outfielder, slides home safely in the ninth inning to score his team's fifth and winning run in the fourth game of the wor series with the Brooklyn Dodgers at Ebbets Field, Brooklyn, New York, Octo 5, 1941. Mickey Owen, the Dodgers catcher who dropped the third strike on Henrich to set up the Yankees' winning drive, has the ball. The Yankees score two more runs in this inning to win 7 to 4. AP PHOTO d Williams (left), Boston Red Sox outfielder, topped the major leagues with a 53 average after the August 18, 1942, Boston Red Sox–New York Yankees game Boston. Here Williams talks over records with Joe DiMaggio, the Yanks' avy-hitting center fielder whose average was then at .311. Both men would soon n the armed forces. AP PHOTO/ABE FOX

▲ New York Yankees outfield and slugger Joe DiMaggio demonstrating his follow-through. Circa 1945. HULT ARCHIVE/GETTY IMAGES

◀ Lou Gehrig, iron-man firs man for the Yankees, playe 2,130 consecutive games. A a great hitter, Gehrig wor many extra hours on his fi technique. WILLIAM C. GRE WORLD-TELEGRAM

(right-handed batters) close to the body helps to guide the bat in a level plane. A batter may lower the plane to hit a ball breaking down or raise it to meet a rising ball, but he must keep the swing level.

The batter begins his swing by cocking his wrists and moving the bat back slightly, then swinging it around his body with the strength of his arms, wrists, and shoulders behind it. As he cocks his wrists he steps toward the pitcher with his left foot and shifts his weight to his left leg, which becomes the axis around which his swing turns. The leg is straight, the knee firm.

The batter must not hurry his swing. The bat must gather speed so that the maximum power is applied as it meets the ball. This means that the batter does not uncock his wrists until almost the instant he connects. The left wrist, for a right-handed batter, guides the bat, and both wrists throw on the power.

Once he hits the ball, the batter must follow through, swinging the bat on until its heavy end has made a big "U" around his shoulders. Remember, the arms *and* the wrists *and* the shoulders give the power. Hurrying the swing and uncocking the wrists too soon cuts off the wrist power. Letting the swing die or failing to follow through cuts off the shoulder power.

The stride is one of the most important parts of the swing, for it not only governs the follow-through but rules the transfer of the weight from the right foot to the left foot at the instant the ball is hit. The stride must be exactly right for the batter's individual style and build.

Overstriding is one of the worst batting flaws and one of the most difficult to correct. A batter who overstrides not only can't pivot for a follow-through but also is thrown off balance as he tries to connect.

Some batters stride as much as 18 inches. My own stride is about 10 inches. Vernon Stephens' stance looks almost spread-eagled, and his stride is no more than 4 or 5 inches. The striding foot should not kick up but should move forward, almost along the ground. The batter who raises his forward leg high as he strides usually is a sucker for a slow-up pitch and often bites at high ones. Mel Ott was the only high strider I ever saw who was a fine hitter.

Mel Ott took an exaggerated stride, and Al Simmons, a great right-handed hitter, hit "bucket-foot"—that is, he pulled his left foot away from the ball as he swung. They played for two of the greatest managers in history—John McGraw and Connie Mack, respectively. The fact that Mr. McGraw and Mr. Mack did not insist on changing their strides indicates that when a player comes up who is naturally a fine hitter in spite of an unorthodox style it is a good thing to let nature alone.

The young player who is developing a style, however, should ask himself, "How many Otts or Simmonses are there? While Simmons, bucket-foot and all, was murdering American League pitching, dozens of other hitters came along who stepped in the bucket and stepped down into the minors. As Lefty Gomez said about a bucket-foot rookie at the Yankees' training camp in St. Petersburg, "He's hitting with one foot in the American Association." In a few weeks the boy was on his way to Kansas City and from there dropped out of sight.

Perhaps the most unorthodox hitter in baseball was Jay Kirke, who played for Joe McCarthy at Louisville. Kirke had a couple of major-league trials but didn't stay up, principally because he couldn't hit the curve.

One day in Philadelphia (so the story goes) he was on deck waiting to hit when the batter ahead of him belted a two-bagger, scoring a man from first. As the relay came in from the outfield Kirke stepped up in front of the catcher and smacked the ball out of the park.

"First fast ball I've seen in a month," he explained.

McCarthy says Kirke would swing at anything his bat could reach and was the best bad-ball hitter he ever saw. Joe says he saw Kirke hit a home run over the center-field fence on a pitch that bounced in front of the plate.

There have been some good hitters in the majors who had the brawn to overpower bad pitches. Joe Medwick, when he first came to the Cardinals, was a famous bad-ball hitter. Batting against Gomez in an All-Star game, he got a home run on a ball so far over his head that he had to jump to hit it. Bill Dickey, who was catching, said he didn't think he could have caught the pitch.

But like Simmons with his foot in the bucket, the successful bad-ball hitters are the exceptions. A batter who hits at a bad ball is doing exactly what the pitcher wants him to do: he is doing part of the pitcher's work for him. I believe that a batter can get his bat on any ball within reach which he can follow with his eyes from the time it leaves the pitcher's hand until it reaches the plate.

But he shouldn't hit at all such balls. He should hit only at balls which are in the strike zone, balls against which he can get the fat part of his bat. Only rarely can a batter apply any real power against a bad ball, and he is foolish to sacrifice power going after them. In judging pitches a batter calls on his "stereoscopic vision." Ted Williams gets as many walks because of his keen eye for balls and strikes as he does because pitchers are deliberately giving him a base on balls.

There is one batting skill that can be developed through practice, and it is the one play in which many amateurs and semipros are superior to major-leaguers. It's the bunt, which should be the simplest play but is bungled frequently by players who have been in the big leagues for years. More close games have been lost because a batter couldn't bunt at the right time than for any other reason.

The main reason the average bunter fails is that he refuses to give himself up. Instead of bunting just to advance the base runner, the batter bunts with the idea in mind of beating it out for a base hit, bunting and running at the same time.

On a bunt the batter has to shift his grip, but he must never

THE BUNT: SLIDE OUTER HAND HALF WAY UP BAT; HOLD BAT LOOSELY AND PARALLEL TO THE GROUND.

shift it before the ball is pitched, for that would be a sure tip-off to the pitcher. Hold the bat loosely and as the pitcher delivers get the bat parallel to the ground, sliding the upper hand halfway up the bat and using the lower hand as a guide. The idea is to make the blow as soft as possible. A tight grip means a fast bunt, which defeats the entire purpose of the play, which is to delay the fielding of the ball to give the runner or runners time to advance. Let the ball hit the bat, don't push at the ball.

Little good can come of bunting at a bad ball. A bunt against a high ball is almost a cinch to be a pop-up. Pick out a good pitch to bunt, unless the situation (such as a squeeze play) demands that the ball must be hit. Knowing the setup is for a bunt, the pitcher naturally will try to get the batter to go for bad pitches; passing them up will force the pitcher to come in with a good one eventually, or else give up a walk. "Three and one" is an excellent spot in which to bunt.

Bunting for a base hit is far different from bunting for a sacrifice to advance the runner. In bunting for a base hit the batter must get a flying start to beat the play, but here too he must be sure to bunt the ball before he starts charging down to first. If he charges on a miss it's a tip-off of what he's trying to do. A left-hander can actually be in motion as he bunts.

Red Rolfe was one of the best bunters I ever saw, mainly because he could disguise his intentions. He was also skillful at placing bunts, which is important for any bunt and is absolutely necessary when the batter is bunting for a base hit. And, batting left-handed, Rolfe was closer to first base from the start.

The drag is an exaggerated bunt. The ball is bunted between the pitcher and first base with too much speed to give the pitcher time to get off the mound and field it and not enough to give the second baseman time to field it and make the play.

It is especially effective with fast, left-handed pull-hitters, when the second baseman plays deep. An occasional drag bunt by such a hitter helps to keep the second baseman "honest," that is, makes him play in his normal position. Right-handed hitters can get away with the drag occasionally, but they must push the ball between the pitcher and first baseman. On drag plays the batter can be in motion before the ball is hit.

Since Babe Ruth introduced the home-run era, and baseball adopted the livelier ball, choke-hitters have practically disappeared from the game. A choke-hitter, taking a short grip, can manipulate the bat better for placing hits but gives up the leverage necessary for long-ball hitting.

While the choke-hitter can, as Willie Keeler said, "hit 'em where they ain't," the best a swing-batter can do in placing hits is to hit them where the ball is. A right-handed swinger can hit an outside pitch to right field; a left-hander can hit an outside pitch to left field.

Swinger or choke-hitter, when ordered to hit behind the runner (that is, to right field when a man is on first base), the hitter must remember that he must sacrifice distance for direction unless the pitch is where he can hit it to right without giving up any power—inside to a left-hander, outside to a right-hander.

Despite all baseball's rules and regulations against "dusters," the fact is that there are times when a pitcher throws at a batter. He doesn't do it with the idea of deliberately injuring the batter, which would be criminal, but with the intention of driving the batter away from the plate and shattering his confidence. As a batter I say a duster is never justified, but maybe a few pitchers could find an excuse for throwing one.

Some pitchers argue that the main reason for a duster is to keep the batter from getting a toe hold at the plate, digging in and getting a firm foot base from which to swing. The average player who has been dusted off usually is foot-loose on his next swing, set to duck away from a close pitch and swinging at the ball with only his arms and without the power of his body behind the swing.

The player who goes to bat afraid of being hit will never be a good hitter. A plate-shy batter pulls away from the ball or rocks back on his heels and can't possibly land on a pitch over the outside corner. He can help himself to overcome his fear by remembering that there have been few serious injuries from pitched balls, and that there are few pitchers vicious enough to try to brain him.

Batters who are "guess hitters" are the ones in constant danger of being beaned, and through no fault of the pitchers. The guess hitter thinks he has the sign for a pitch and, anticipating a curve, comes up to the front of the box to hit it before it breaks. If he guesses wrong, or has been misinformed by a coach or runner, and the pitch happens to be a fast ball, he has to hit the dirt to keep from being skulled.

There are some coaches who are clever at stealing signs and letting the batter know what's coming, but I prefer to pick out my own pitch to hit. I'd rather trust my own eyes than make up my mind in advance, or have it made up for me, that the next one is going to be a fast ball or a curve. There's always the chance that the coach has miscued, or that the pitcher has gotten onto his sign by stealing and is crossing him up.

This is not to say that the batter should reject any tip-off which the pitcher gives as to what's coming next. If a pitcher has some betraying mannerism, such as patting the mound or picking up a handful of dirt before throwing a curve ball, the batter should certainly take advantage of it; but he should always bear in mind that he may be guessing wrong.

There has been much discussion of the over-shifted defense since the Cleveland Indians went into their famous "Boudreau shift" against Ted Williams halfway through the 1946 season. When the Cardinals, adopting a variation of it, bottled him up in the World Series that year he was heavily criticized for not finding a way to combat the shift.

The success of the over-shifted defense against Williams in the 1946 World Series was, to my mind, just an exceptional case of a special defense rigged up to stop a particular hitter. Williams happened to have a bad Series. Certainly no over-shifting prevented him from walking away with all batting honors in the American League in 1947, and over a 154-game stretch.

Williams is a great hitter, one of the best in the whole history of baseball, and he reached this place by pulling the ball to right field and hitting it a long way. A good swing is a grooved swing, and Williams's is grooved for long, pulled hits.

By constantly trying to poke the ball into left field, away from the shifted defense, he would have lost his groove, wrecked his timing and ruined himself as a slugger. But no good hitter should let the defense get away with over-shifting for long. Without upsetting his swing he can shorten up occasionally and belt one for the spot which the over-shift leaves open, crossing up the defense, just as Williams did when he laid down a bunt toward unprotected third base in the 1946 Series. But time after time Williams is sent up there to hit the long ball to right field, the performance which is expected of him.

The Dodgers over-shifted against me in the 1947 World Series. I attempted a couple of pokes to the weak side but didn't get away with it, so I had to combat the special defense with my natural swing. I'm signed up as a power hitter to left field and couldn't run the risk of changing my entire batting style by trying to push the ball toward right.

One question that many fans ask about batting is whether the pressure is on the hitter or the pitcher in a tight spot in the game. It's the last half of the ninth, the bases are loaded, the count on the batter is three and two; everybody is going to run with the pitch; a walk will tie the score and probably will bring in the winning run. Who's on the spot—the pitcher or the hitter?

Who has the most confidence? If the pitcher is a good, cool competitor, a Joe Page, a Hugh Casey, with stuff and control, and the batter isn't reliable in the clutch, the pressure is certainly on the hitter. If the pitcher is wild, wobbly, and weak in the knees, and the hitter is a Henrich or a Slaughter, the heat is surely on the pitcher.

If it's a fine pitcher and a fine hitter, say a Hubbell against a Gehringer, the pressure is on neither of them; they are just two good workmen up there, confident of doing a job. If the hitter hits, it's just what he expected; if he goes out, the pitcher is not surprised.

When I was with the San Francisco Seals, Walter "Duster" Mails, who pitched for Cleveland in the 1920 World Series against the Dodgers, was still an active player in our league. One day when he had the count at three and two on a batter, he turned to the stands and calmly announced, "Ladies and gentlemen, this is what we pitchers call the difficult pitch." And he struck the batter out.

12: Pitching Procedure

THE PITCHER is the man who bars the door, using his arm as the latch. He has the most exhausting job in baseball. He scrimmages personally with every batter on the opposing team. His work usually determines whether each game is baseball or burlesque.

I think all successful pitchers are born pitchers, for I have never known one who didn't have a fast ball. The fast ball is a natural gift, which no amount of practice will develop. Whenever an infielder or an outfielder is made over into a pitcher, it's the fast ball that puts him on that track. It was Bucky Walters's lightning throws across the infield that led Jimmy Wilson to turn him into a pitcher. It was the hard pegs that Clint Hartung turned loose from the outfield that made Mel Ott experiment with him on the mound in 1947.

Control is as important in successful pitching as the fast ball. It is obtainable through practice, especially if the pitcher is intelligent and observant and isn't afraid of hard work.

With a fast ball and control, a pitcher has more than two-thirds of his requirements for success. He can pick up the other pitching refinements as he goes along and develop the extra pitches to augment his control and speed. But no matter how much stuff a pitcher may have, it's worthless if he can't make it go where he wants.

Control must be mastered by degrees. The initial target is a rectangle 12 inches at the base and about 39 inches high. Twelve inches is the width of the plate. Thirty-nine inches is about the distance from shoulder to knee on a man around 5 feet 10 inches tall. Over the plate and between the batter's shoulder and knees is the strike zone. The pitching distance is 60 feet 6 inches.

The pitcher first must concentrate on getting his fast ball across the plate. He must be able to do it consistently, and in the strike zone. Then he can take on the job of learning spot pitching—working the corners or getting the ball over high or low. His fast ball is his natural pitch, and once he has learned to control that pitch he can go on to his curve and his change of pace. Sometimes a pitcher who is just missing the plate may improve his control by changing his position on the pitching rubber, which is 2 feet wide. By experimenting he may find that he can hit the target from a certain position off the center of the rubber.

Big-league pitchers constantly are asked, "How do you hold your fast ball?" or "How do you hold your curve?" In baseball talk, the way the pitcher holds the ball for a particular pitch is called "fingering." Fingering, however, is only one of several factors that can cause the ball to act in a specific way on a specific pitch. Freddy Fitzsimmons, a great knuckle-baller for fifteen years in the National League, tried to teach his knuckler to teammates on the Giants and the Dodgers and, later, the Phillies, when he managed them. Of all his pupils Larry French alone achieved a real standout knuckler, and French was a veteran when he learned the pitch. He not only fingered the ball as Fitzsimmons did, but learned to deliver it with a stiff wrist, just as Fitzsimmons threw it. The others could not overcome the habit of snapping the wrist.

The fingering for a fast ball is the natural grip on a baseball. Pick up a ball as if you were going to throw it hard. You will find that automatically you have gripped it around its equator with the forefinger and second finger on top, the thumb on the bottom, and the third finger and little finger folded down against the palm.

The pitcher lets his fast one go straight off his fingers toward the plate, without a twist to left or right. The axis of the ball is parallel to the ground and at a right angle to a line between the pitcher's hand and the plate. A good fast ball rises as it approaches the plate—the "hop on the fast one."

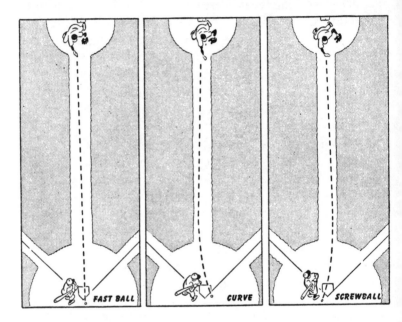

The fingering for fast ball and curve are the same, but the curve is delivered with a sharp outward snap of the wrist that turns the back of the hand toward the plate. The pitcher lets the ball go off the forefinger.

A curve ball spins toward the first-base side of the plate if thrown by a right-handed pitcher, toward the third-base side if thrown by a left-hander. In other words, a right-hander's curve breaks away from a right-handed batter, a left-hander's curve breaks away from a left-handed batter.

A curve ball breaking away from a hitter usually is more difficult to hit than a ball breaking toward him. This explains the "percentage" of sending a left-handed pinch hitter up to bat against a right-handed pitcher, or a right-hander to bat against a southpaw.

The first right-handed batter to face Carl Hubbell's screwball must have been caught as flatfooted as a G.I. after a 12-mile march. A curve ball from a left-hander breaking away from a right-handed batter! That's how the screwball, called the "fadeaway" in Christy Mathewson's day, behaves, and I've never heard of any pitcher who could control it like Mathewson and Hubbell.

The fingering for curve ball and screwball is the same, but the screwball is delivered with a terrific inward snap of the wrist that turns the palm of the hand toward the plate. Hubbell got tremendous spin on the screwball by flicking it with the forefinger just before it took off from the second finger.

The screwball puts a terrific strain on the pitcher's elbow, and no one should try it until he has learned the fundamentals of pitching and has sense enough to be careful of arm strain. The effect on Hubbell of his famous delivery is noticeable today. When he stands relaxed, with his arms hanging at his sides, the palm of his left hand faces out.

The average equipment of a pitcher is a fast ball, a curve ball and a change of pace. Change of pace, or letup pitch, means a ball thrown at less than normal speed.

Fingering and delivery motion for the fast ball and the slow ball are exactly the same. In pitching the slow ball, however, the two top fingers are lifted from the ball as it leaves the hand. Its entire effect depends on its being delivered with exactly the same motion as the fast ball. Expecting a fast ball, the batter will be swinging on it before it gets up to the plate. The slow curve is delivered with the same outward wrist snap as the ordinary curve ball, but the two top fingers are lifted as the ball leaves the hand. It breaks less sharply than the ordinary curve.

A pitcher who has a good stock of fast ball, curve, and change of pace is a very good pitcher indeed, usually a twenty-game winner. Not content with all this, pitchers have gone out and developed what they call "the extra pitch," such as the slider, the knuckler, the butterfly ball, the fork ball, or the sinker.

There are three ways to finger the knuckle ball. The most popular is to grip the ball with the first joints of forefinger and second finger on top. Another way is to place the first joint of the first three fingers on top of the ball. A third grip is with only the tips of the fingers on top. Fitzsimmons delivers it with a stiff wrist. The ball does not spin and usually takes such a sharp dip that it looks as if it suddenly has dropped straight down.

The butterfly ball is a variation of the knuckle ball, the difference being that it is delivered with a sharp wrist snap, as in the curve or slow ball. It dips and also breaks in or out, depending on the wrist motion. Many pitchers in the majors can't tell whether it will break in or out when it leaves their hand, and it takes a capable catcher to handle this pitch.

In fingering the fork ball the first and second fingers are held wide apart, with the ball gripped tightly between them and resting on the thumb. It is delivered with the fast-ball motion, but its speed is much less and it does not rotate. It dips but does not break to either side.

The sinker is a fast ball, usually delivered underhand, and breaks downward sharply as it approaches the plate. Some pitchers have succeeded in delivering an overhand sinker, which breaks to left or right and is even more deceptive because of its novelty.

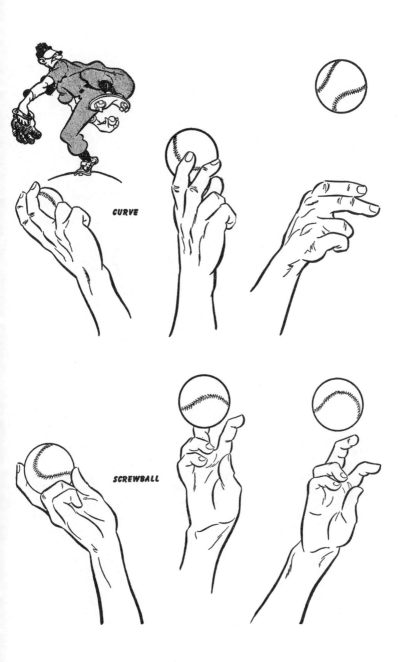

CURVE

SCREWBALL

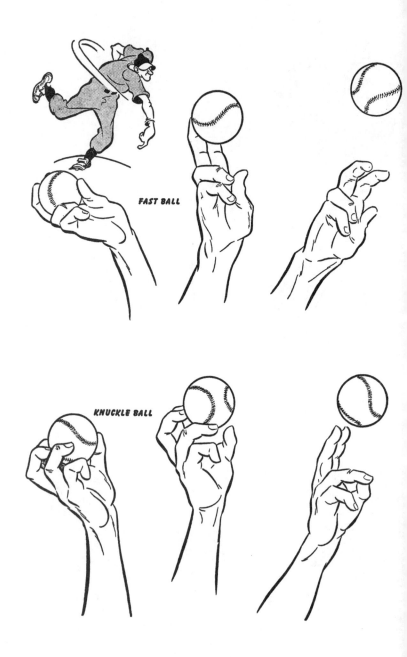

FAST BALL

KNUCKLE BALL

The slider is delivered like the fast ball, but with a slight wrist twist. It behaves somewhat like a curve but seems to slide rather than break away from the hitter and does not break downward. To throw a slider some pitchers grip the ball slightly off the equator.

The palm ball is gripped with all four fingers on top, the thumb underneath, and the ball shoved back against the palm. As with all change-of-pace pitches, which are intended to throw the batter off his timing, it must be delivered with the same motion as the fast ball.

Whatever the pitch, don't let the batter know what's coming in advance. Make him find out for himself in that fraction of a second that the ball is traveling down to the plate. Surprise and deception are two major allies of the pitcher. Use the glove at all times to hide the fingering from the batter, his coaches, and his teammates on base, and avoid mannerisms that tip them off. Some coaches are magicians at stealing pitches as well as signs. Art Fletcher was one of the best. Del Baker, Mike Gonzales, and Charley Dressen are other experts at it.

Burleigh Grimes, the old spitballer, was one of the very best in the business, but when Fletcher was with the Phillies they used to plaster him. Wilbert Robinson, Grimes's manager on the Dodgers, thought the Phils were stealing the signs from the catcher. In Baker Bowl he put a sentry in the center-field clubhouse to see if a spotter with field glasses was getting the signs and relaying them to the batter.

As a spitballer Grimes had to pretend that he was moistening the ball every time he threw, or else he would give away the pitch. Sharp-eyed Fletcher noticed that Grimes wore a tight cap and that when he actually moistened the ball his jaw muscles moved so that the cap peak worked up and down. "Boy" was the sign for the spitter. When Fletcher saw the cap peak move he shouted "Come on, boy!" or "You can do it, Bill, old boy!" and the hitter was all set for the pitch.

Whatever his natural talents may be, a pitcher can use them more effectively by using them strategically. The top strategy is to "mix 'em up." Only a few—Walter Johnson, Lefty Grove, Bob Feller—have been able to succeed simply by blasting the ball past the hitters. And none get by entirely on curve balls. In fact, old-timers insist that if John McGraw had any single weakness as a manager it was his insistence that his pitchers throw only number two, the curve ball, in the clutch. Good hitters opposing the Giants learned to anticipate it. It takes a great pitcher to give the batter what he expects and still get him out.

Here are two examples of smart pitching, with me as the goat. In the fifth inning of the last game of the 1942 World Series against the Cardinals, the Yankees had the bases filled and two out when I came to bat against Johnny Beazley. On my previous turn against him I had singled home the run which put us ahead. I had been hitting his fast ball pretty well and figured I would see no more fast ones from him.

He threw me two low curves. One of them got a corner for a strike. I was waiting for more of the same. He fooled me by coming in with a fast one. It was close, but I felt I could not let it go by. I fell back a bit as I hit and didn't get the fat part of the bat on the ball. The result was a grounder to Whitey Kurowski at third for a force-out to end the inning.

This was a perfect example of the pitcher outfiguring the hitter. Beazley counted on me to look for the curve and knew I'd jump at the fast ball.

In the fifth game of the 1947 World Series against the Dodgers, I went to bat against Hugh Casey and hit into a double play on one of the finest curve balls I have ever seen. This ball started to come in about letter-high, then broke for the outside corner. I was able to follow it all right and was halfway through my swing when I realized that this was no ordinary curve ball and that it was going to break about 6 inches farther away than I had expected. I tried to check my swing, but it was too late. The ball hit my bat for what may have been the easiest double play in World Series history.

The pitcher was thinking right along with the hitter. Because the bases were filled Casey was a cinch to feed me curves in the hope of getting me to hit on the ground. Where he foxed me was by giving me this extra-special curve that I hadn't seen before. If I had laid off, it would have been a ball, but I thought I had the curve gauged perfectly. Instead, Casey had me gauged perfectly.

Here is another example of pitching judgment, or lack of it. In an exhibition game against the Giants, a Yankee pitcher threw a home-run ball to Phil Weintraub with the bases filled. He was so sore that he burned three pitches over to strike the next batter out.

"What did you give Weintraub?" Joe McCarthy asked him.

"Change of pace."

"What did you throw for the strike-out?"

"Fast sinker."

"That's right," McCarthy said with mild sarcasm. "Always save your best one for after the damage is done."

Some pitchers increase their effectiveness by altering their delivery on certain pitches. A pitcher who employs a three-quarter overhand motion, the most usual pitching motion, can distract some hitters by switching to sidearm. It is effective only when both pitcher and batter are right-handed or left-handed. To a right-handed hitter, a sidearm pitch from a right-handed pitcher seems to be coming by way of third base. A hitter who is the least bit gun-shy can be confused and thrown entirely off by this pitch, which to him seems as if it were thrown from a point behind his head. Much of Ewell Blackwell's success with Cincinnati may be traced to the manner in which he delivers overhand to left-handed hitters.

In general, however, delivery of fast ball, curve ball, and change of pace with the same motion is the foundation of deception and surprise.

Timing of deliveries is an important factor in clever pitching. Pitchers should be careful not to become so regular in their delivery that the batter can time the pitch in advance. By varying the time between pitches, the deception is increased. And no pitcher should hurry his deliveries unless he is faced with the threat of rain, darkness, or some other condition which demands that the half-inning be ended as quickly as possible.

The batter's style and stance must have a bearing on the manner of pitching to him. A batter who holds the bat at the very end, arms well away from the body, usually can be pitched to inside, across the letters of his shirt, since he can't get the full power of his swing against such a pitch. A batter who takes a long stride forward often is fooled by a change of pace or a high ball, above the strike zone. Low and outside is the spot to pitch to bucket-foot hitters.

Many schoolboy pitchers fall into the bad habit of "cunnythumbing" their curve ball, which means that the thumb sticks out from the ball as they grip it. Cunny-thumbing not only is unnatural and unrelaxed but is a dead giveaway.

A pitcher's arm is his meal ticket, and he can't be blamed if he babies it and coddles it. He runs his biggest risk of suffering a sore arm if he tries to pitch without a sufficient warm-up. Almost as dangerous is to have his arm "cool out" between innings. That is why he puts on his jacket when he gets on base and why he puts it over his throwing arm when he sits in the dugout.

Some pitchers can warm up more quickly than others. This

is true of all the first-flight relief pitchers, such as Johnny Murphy, Joe Page, Hugh Casey. Even when Johnny Murphy was a veteran with the Yankees, he could warm up more quickly than most of the younger men in the American League. Practice should determine how long a pitcher requires to get his arm thoroughly loosened. Many a pitcher has lost a game by his work against the first few batters because he was not sufficiently warmed up when he took the mound. A pitcher can tell by his warm-up pitches when he is really ready to work effectively.

With a few notable exceptions, such as Murphy, a pitcher usually requires more time to warm up as he grows older. Ted Lyons, near the end of his active career as a pitcher for the White Sox, always began his warming-up drill about five minutes sooner than he did in his younger days. The object of the warm-up, of course, is to get the arm thoroughly loosened before attempting to put anything on the ball.

Some pitchers believe that night air is injurious to their pitching arms and take extra precautions when working night games. Night games are now a common practice, and no pitcher, however he feels about them, can go through a season without working his share of them. It certainly seems logical that a cold afternoon in April carries more of a threat to a pitcher's arm than a Turkish-bath evening in August.

A pitcher's style on the mound is important not only to the pitch itself but to his capacity for fielding batted balls and for holding runners on base.

A full windup should be taken whenever conditions permit, for it increases the effectiveness and deception of the pitch. It is a good idea to stand behind the rubber until the catcher gives the sign. The pitcher must deliver the ball from the rubber. With nobody on base, both feet are in contact with the rubber as the windup starts. To illustrate with a right-handed pitcher, the heel of the right foot is on the rubber, the toes of the left foot touching its rear edge.

As the (right-handed) pitcher draws back his arm to throw the ball, the entire weight of his body is thrown on his right foot, which is on the rubber. Movement of his body as he rears back brings his left foot off the ground, his left hand extended in front of him as a balance. The left foot strides forward as the pitching arm begins to whip toward the plate, and is planted on the ground, the entire weight shifting onto it at the instant the ball leaves the pitcher's fingers. Thus the force of the entire body is behind the pitch. Then comes the follow-through, as important to a pitcher as to a batter. The right foot comes forward alongside the left, toes of both feet pointing to the plate, body bent forward slightly, weight evenly distributed.

The delivery is a three-step motion. One: rear back on the right leg (right-handed pitchers); two: stride forward with left foot and plant it as the ball is thrown; three: bring the right foot even and recover balance, ready to break quickly in any direction for a batted ball. A pitcher who doesn't recover his balance quickly not only is handicapped in fielding but even in protecting himself from injury by a hard smash through the box. A correct follow-through can be developed by practice. Fritz Ostermueller is a good example: he had real trouble squaring off after the pitch when he first came up with the Red Sox, but he put in a lot of hard work at it and acquired the knack.

A pitcher who hesitates, or breaks his motion, once he has started his windup is, of course, guilty of a balk. So is a pitcher who throws to a base without taking a step in the direction of that base or a pitcher who, with his foot on the rubber, feints a throw to a base and does not complete it. It is a balk if a pitcher, having started his windup, doesn't come to a perceptible pause as he joins both hands together, preparatory to delivering the ball to the plate.

Much of the pitcher's effectiveness comes from his ability to hold men on base. Southpaws naturally have a big advantage over right-handers in holding the runner on first, since the play is directly in front of them, not behind them. In holding the runner on second, there is one good rule to follow: right-handers wheel to the left, left-handers wheel to the right, to make the throw. Some pitchers, even in the major leagues, lose valuable time wheeling the wrong way.

With a man on first, the right-handed pitcher delivers with the right heel on the rubber. With a man on second, he contacts the rubber with the outside of the right foot, the toe toward third base.

Some pitchers have deliberately set out to develop a motion for holding batters on first that is just within the law on balks. It consists of lifting the leg as if to start the stride toward the plate, but striding instead toward the base. These tricky pitchers almost always catch the runner leading toward second.

Sherry Smith, the former Brooklyn pitcher, was reputed to have this trick down so pat that after he had drifted to the minors he would occasionally walk a tough hitter rather than pitch to him, then pick him off at first.

Larry French, pitching for the Cubs, picked Frenchy Bordagaray off second in an extra-inning game at Ebbets Field while Bordagaray was standing almost on top of the bag, nervously tapping it with his toe.

"You were practically standing on the base, tapping it with your toe. How did he pick you off?" demanded Casey Stengel, Bordagaray's manager.

"I dunno," Frenchy said. "He must have got me between taps."

Bobby Feller was green at holding runners on base when he broke in with Cleveland, and he probably lost as many games for this reason as for any other, including his early lack of control. It is a real tribute to his intelligence that he could overcome this weakness. Some pitchers never do. Feller has a peculiar stride, in that he steps toward third instead of the plate as he delivers the ball. He worked long and hard to learn how to hold the runner on base.

One great pitcher who was never able to hold runners on base was Dazzy Vance, the strike-out king of the Dodgers. He told Manager Robinson that if he watched the runner on first he lost his eye and his control. It was tough on his battery mate, Hank DeBerry, but DeBerry was philosophical about it as long as Vance continued to win. When someone stole second he would say to Vance, "Don't worry about it. That steal is only a loan."

On most bunts which the pitcher fields, the catcher will be close by, ready to shout at which base the play should be made. Pitchers rarely get a chance to make a force play on an attempted sacrifice, since the average bunt fielded by the pitcher is so well placed that the base runners have plenty of time to beat the play. The pitcher can dig a real hole for himself if he tries for a force at second or third and gets nobody. It's wise to listen to the shouted instructions of the catcher, who has the play in front of him.

A pitcher who gives bunt situations a little thought in advance helps himself a lot. He ought to have an accurate idea of the speed of the runner already on base, so that if he fields the ball he can judge soundly what chance he has to make the play elsewhere than at first.

Pitchers must learn to break from the rubber automatically and to start to first on all fair balls hit to the first-base side. If the first baseman fields the ball, the pitcher has to cover the base. The pitcher who gets a good jump on the play makes it simple for himself. For one thing, he can take the throw from the first baseman a step or two ahead of the bag, which means he will have no trouble locating it.

When a runner is on first, the pitcher should back up third base on all balls hit to the outfield. With a runner on second he should back up the catcher on outfield clouts.

Naturally, the better a pitcher hits and fields the easier he makes his main task. It often works out that the better the pitcher, the better all-around ballplayer he is. Dizzy Dean could hit, field, and run bases. Red Ruffing could hit and field, and, heavy as he is, I've seen him beat out slow rollers for base hits in World Series games just because he hustled at every opportunity. Freddy Fitzsimmons was such a good fielder that he made up a five-man infield for his teams.

Lots of fans ask ballplayers what goes on in those conferences on the mound. Sometimes the catcher goes out to say, "You're not bearing down," or the manager comes over for a "Pitch to him like this," or, "You feel O.K.?" It was just such a conversation that Manager Bill Terry had with Adolfo Luque in the eleventh inning of the final game of the 1933 World Series between the Giants and the Senators at Washington.

The Senators had two out, Joe Kuhel was up, and the count was two balls and two strikes. Terry walked over from first and said, "Are you sure you're all right, Dolf? This is an important pitch. All we have to do is get this guy out. I've got Hubbell warming up. You sure you're O.K.?"

"See you in the clubhouse," Luque said, and struck the batter out on the next pitch.

13: Base Running

For EVERYONE who plays baseball and everyone who wants to watch it with understanding, there is one thing to remember about base running—speed isn't everything. It certainly helps, but on many ball clubs the fastest man is by no means the best base runner. Knowing when to run is the most important ingredient of base running.

A good base runner combines speed, intelligence, sharp powers of observation, and, surprising as it may seem, reputation. A player who has a reputation as a good base runner worries the defense the minute he gets on base.

Brooklyn offered two perfect examples of the value of a base-running reputation with Pete Reiser in 1946 and Jackie Robinson in 1947. In 1946 Reiser stole home seven times. Consequently, every time Reiser got on third the pitcher worked with one eye on him and one eye on the batter. In 1947, Robinson, taking a long lead off first or dancing up and down the base lines, was a constant headache to National League pitchers. And his base-running skill didn't help the Yankees any during the World Series.

Branch Rickey has always been one of the foremost exponents of speed and dash on the base paths and he found a strong supporter when he named Billy Southworth to manage the Cardinals. Southworth believes firmly that speed has psychological advantages as well as material benefits.

"If you have fast men on your club," he says, "you should promote that advantage to the hilt. Get the men in the habit of rounding the base on every hit, of taking the extra base whenever possible. This can cause misplays in the outfield and the infield by making the defense overanxious. The fielders are hurried, rush their throws, try to field ground balls too quickly. The first thing you know they're giving you the chance to take the extra base."

A speedy, aggressive, hustling club always puts extra pressure on the defense. A player should remember that he becomes a base runner the instant he moves out from home plate. He should run out every hit full speed even if it seems to be an easy out; it is sometimes as easy to boot big, hopping grounders and to drop soft flies as it is to muff the difficult put-outs. If ball four is wild, he should tear down to first, not jog; there's the chance he might be able to get an extra base. He should be alert to a missed third strike, just as Tommy Henrich was in the World Series of 1941.

When the batter gets a hit which seems to be no more than an ordinary single to the outfield, he should not just run down to first and let it go at that. He should run hard and make his turn, that is, pivot toward second to be in position to take the extra base in the event of a fumble, a bad throw, or a throw to the wrong base.

On hits to the outfield, the batter should start his run for first from outside the foul line. (A runner may go out of the base line without penalty at any time except when he does so to avoid being put out.) By approaching first from outside the foul line, he is in a position to pivot toward second with far less waste motion than if he runs directly down the base line.

In making his turn the runner should tag first base with his left foot, hitting the inside corner and putting the step with his right foot on a direct line with second. In this way he keeps from making too wide a turn at first. All bases, in fact, should be tagged with the left foot for this reason, but the runner should never change his stride just to do it.

On extra-base hits the player should watch the coaches first, the ball later. If the hit is a long drive to the outfield, the coach at first base hand-signals him to make his turn. As the player rounds first the coach shouts instructions as to whether he is to hold up or to try for two bases.

Charging from first to second, the runner can judge for him-

MAKING THE TURN AT FIRST — LEFT
FOOT HITS INSIDE CORNER OF BAG.

self whether he will have to slide or whether he has a chance to round the base and possibly go on to third.

If he makes the turn at second, he takes instructions from the coach at third as to whether to come on or to hold up. A runner advancing from second to third should always be under the third-base coach's directions. If he turns and tries to locate the ball himself, he will lose speed and break stride.

In addition to the coaching signals, the runner must at all times watch the runner ahead of him. Forgetting the man ahead can lead into terrible bonehead plays and cause disastrous traffic jams. Tom Meany, with whom I am collaborating in this book, was official scorer of the Dodger-Braves game at Ebbets Field in 1926, in which the most spectacular pile-up in the history of baseball took place. The generally accepted version of this play is that Babe Herman tripled into a triple play that wound up with three Dodgers on third base. Even Bob Ripley, the collector of *Believe-It-or-Not* oddities, reported it this way. Meany says it was bad enough, but not that bad.

He reports, "Herman didn't triple into a triple play. He only, if you'll pardon the expression, doubled into a double play. It couldn't have been a triple play because there already was one out when Herman came to bat with the bases filled.

"Hank DeBerry was on third, Dazzy Vance on second, and Chick Fewster on first. Babe really tied into one and hit it on a line against the wall in right. DeBerry, of course, scored easily, and Vance should have scored too, but Vance was a big man and not very fast. He rounded third all right, but decided there was a chance of being caught at the plate by the relay and he pulled up to come back to the plate. Fewster had rounded second and was halfway to third when he saw Vance stop, so Chick pulled up, too. Not Herman, however. Babe went flying past Fewster without even seeing him and slid into third from one side just as Vance slid in from the other. And the ball arrived about that time, too. Fewster took one look at the situation and disgustedly walked in to short right to retrieve his glove and take his fielding position at second base. As far as he was concerned, the inning was over.

"The relay was taken by Eddie Taylor, playing third base for the Braves. He tagged Herman and Vance, in that order, and looked at Ernie Quigley, who was umpiring at third, expecting to see him jerk his thumb indicating that one or the other was out. Quigley gave no sign, so Taylor tagged them all over again, in reverse order. Again no sign from Quigley.

"The fact is that Herman was already out for passing Fewster, the runner ahead of him, so tagging him meant nothing. And tagging Vance meant nothing, either, since he was entitled to third base, for the player with whom he was sharing it was already out.

"Doc Gautreau, another Braves infielder, got the idea and he grabbed the ball from Taylor and started for Fewster, who was walking around nonchalantly in the vicinity of second base. When Chick saw Doc coming after him he ran for his life and finally was tagged out in the bull pen in right field. Of course he was out as soon as he started away from Gautreau, for he was going out of the base line to avoid being put out. Had Fewster gone back to second base and stayed on the bag, Herman would have been the only out on that play."

Generally, when fans speak of base running they are talking about a player's ability to steal bases. The knack of taking an extra base on a long hit is an equally important part, equally valuable to the offense, and it usually is easier to take an extra base by alert, heads-up running than to steal one.

In stealing bases, the lead is all important. Max Carey, one of the greatest of base stealers, preached it all the time. He argued that it was no more damaging to be picked off first on a long lead than to be thrown out at second because the lead hadn't been long enough. The trick, of course, is not to get picked off or thrown out.

No base runner should take a lead until the pitcher has assumed his position on the rubber. That's sure prevention against being caught by the hidden-ball trick. While the pitcher has the ball the runner should not lead more than two strides and a short slide from the base. Two strides and a short slide should bring him back to base ahead of a throw from the pitcher.

In taking his lead, the runner's weight should be evenly distributed on both feet. If he is leaning toward second with his weight on his right foot, he may find himself picked off; that is the spot the pitchers wait for to try a pick-off. On the other hand, if the weight is on the left foot, the runner cannot get a good jump toward second. It's when he takes his lead off first that the runner gets dividends for being observant. He watches the pitcher's feet, knees, arms, and shoulders to determine the exact instant the ball is going to be delivered. At that instant he breaks toward second, to be in motion if the ball is hit on the ground, or to steal if the play is a steal.

There is no sense in trying to steal second if the runner's team is more than one run behind. Behind by one run or with the score tied, the runner has a chance to put an important run into scoring position by stealing. A steal should be attempted only when the potential tally, which the base runner represents, is an important one. It is rarely good judgment to steal with none out.

If the lead is the most important part of the steal, the slide is just behind it in importance. Because of the physical dangers involved, headfirst sliding is not recommended. There have been some players, notably Pepper Martin, who have been exceptional headfirst sliders, but it is a risky play, inviting anything from a broken finger to a spiked shoulder.

Sliding feet first, the runner has two choices. He can slide into the base on his right leg, hooking the bag with his left toe, or he can come in on his left leg, hooking the bag with his right toe. He should slide to the side away from the fielder, giving him only one foot instead of the whole body as the area to tag.

Picture the play: the runner goes down with the pitch, the catcher fires the ball to second in an effort to nail him. If the throw is in front of the bag, the runner should hit the ground on his right leg and tag the base with his left foot. If the throw is over the bag, he should come in on his left side, making connections with his right toe.

Practice sliding on both sides. Too many players slide only one way, letting the fielder know in advance on which side he

THE SLIDE.

will have to make the tag. Good, cagey base runners often make bluff steals to learn by observation whether the second baseman or the shortstop is going to cover, so that they may plan their slides accordingly.

The leg on which the slide is made must be relaxed. The greatest physical danger in a slide is to have the spikes catch the dirt, making the leg buckle with the entire weight of the body on it. If the leg is stiff, a sprain or a broken leg may result.

Once a runner has made up his mind to slide he must slide. A "half-slide" invites injury. It has disabled many a ballplayer.

There are two reasons for sliding, one to avoid being tagged, the other to prevent overrunning the base. The slide should always be to the side of the base which is farther from the fielder. Don't slide into the fielder, but away from him. Make.him do the tagging. Occasionally I've been able to make a base safely by sliding completely past it and then slapping one hand on it.

Slide into second on all force plays. This prevents overrunning the bag, and if the fielder fumbles the ball or misses the base, the slider is not as open a target for a tag as a runner would be who comes in standing up.

When trapped, a runner should never give himself up when there is a chance to prolong the play with a run-down. This is vital when there are other runners on base, because the longer the run-down is kept going, the more chance the other runners have to advance a base.

The most common double-steal attempt in the majors is with men on first and third. The jump the man on first gets on this play usually determines its success. His job is to go all the way through, just as if there were no runner on third, and to try to make a clean theft of second. There is one exception: if the ball beats him to the bag, he must retreat toward first in the hope of developing a run-down that will give the man on third a chance to break for the plate.

The duties of the man on the third-base end of a double steal are even tougher. He must get a good lead, but not so long a lead that he can be nailed by a catcher who bluffs a throw to second, then whips the ball to third. And if he makes his break for home and is caught because the ball is cut off, he must try to make the run-down so protracted that the man on first has a chance to come all the way around to third.

An important responsibility of the base runner is to break up double plays. This does not mean just sliding into the pivot man, which is routine. It means breaking up the double play by remote control. For instance: runners are on first and third and the batter hits a ball which may be handled for a double play by way of second. The man on third must break toward the plate to draw a throw there and prevent the play at second.

The runner on third should break toward home on any ball hit to the infield (except, of course, a smash at the third baseman), in order to force the defense to play him at the plate. Incidentally, a runner on third base should always stand in foul territory when taking his lead. That prevents any possibility of his being hit by a ball batted fair. Base runners struck by fairly batted balls are automatically out.

Most of the time an attempt to steal home is a foolish risk. It is the most difficult steal of all, and only a good base runner should try it. There are so many other ways to score from third—on any hit, a long fly, a difficult infield chance, an error, a wild pitch, a passed ball, etc.—that the risk involved in an attempted steal home is worth taking only rarely.

When Billy Meyer was appointed manager of Pittsburgh in December, 1947, Casey Stengel, who had managed in the American Association back in the late 1920's, asked him if he was going to teach the Pirates his famous steal home, which he made when he was the playing manager of Louisville and Stengel was managing Toledo.

Meyer tells it this way. "I was the base runner on third base, with the bases filled, two out, and the count on the batter three balls and two strikes. I was getting along in years and couldn't run very fast, and nobody expected me to steal home, so I was able to take a pretty good lead. Just as the pitcher started his windup, I broke for the plate.

"The pitcher saw me, of course, and threw the ball a bit outside, and the catcher had me by so far that I was tagged standing up. The catcher almost broke my ribs putting the ball on me, and the umpire jerked up his thumb and said, 'You're out,' but I took him aside and said, 'Now, don't get excited, Mr. Umpire, but I'm not out. Where did the pitcher throw the ball to the batter? Couple of feet up the line, wasn't it? And that makes the fourth ball on the batter. So, what happens to the runner on third when the batter is walked with the bases filled? He is forced over with a run, isn't he?' "

Meyer, of course, was perfectly correct. The success of such a play depends upon startling the pitcher, so that he momentarily forgets his situation at the plate—that the count is three and two on the batter—and throws outside to enable the catcher to tag the runner. The defense against the play is made by the pitcher's stepping back off the rubber, provided he can do so without balking, and then pitching out to the catcher, since a pitch made under these conditions doesn't affect the count. Otherwise the pitcher must get the ball in the strike zone.

Base running often is called "daring" when it is merely reckless. A runner should always remember that intelligence is as important as speed. It is reckless to take chances with none out, but there are times when it is intelligent to take the same chance with two out. A runner on a team which is trailing by a couple of runs should never take chances, except in the late innings, because the run he represents means nothing by itself.

A runner with the base immediately ahead of him occupied usually can get a good lead because the defense knows that a steal is impossible. Runners who find themselves in this situation should take advantage of it, getting a good lead, but always being alert not to be caught sleeping by a pick-off play. A runner who knows he isn't being watched often starts daydreaming.

There are two fairly common situations in baseball in which an alert, speedy base runner can help the offense tremendously. One is in stretching a long single to a double, and the other is in going from first to third on an ordinary outfield single. Stretching the long single to a two-bagger eliminates the danger of the double-play hazard which is always present when there is a runner on first base. It also puts the runner in scoring position.

Going from first to third on a single likewise eliminates a double-play threat and frequently makes it possible for the batter, too, to take an extra base. The man going from first to third on an ordinary single forces the outfielder to make a play on him, and on the throw to third the batsman has a chance to go from first to second.

It is in plays like these, rather than in stolen bases, that the over-all speed of a club and its base-running skill is apparent. It was what Billy Southworth meant when he spoke of fast, hustling teams exerting pressure on the defense.

The Yankees opened and closed the World Series of 1939 with some alert baseball which was a big factor in sweeping the four games against Cincinnati. Joe Gordon's great base running tied up the first game for us at a time when Paul Derringer had us trailing by 1 to 0. With one out in the fifth, Gordon singled. Babe Dahlgren, who that season had replaced Lou Gehrig at first base for us, hit what looked like a long single to left. Gordon, of course, was a cinch to go from first to third on the hit, but Babe had his head up, too, and rounded first to stretch the hit to a double. Wally Berger, playing left field for the Reds, made a long throw to second to head off Dahlgren. Art Fletcher, the Yankees' coach at third base, waved Gordon on in to the plate, and Joe slid in with the tying run, under the relay throw. It was heads-up work by Gordon, Dahlgren, and Fletcher.

In the fourth game of the Series, a Cincinnati infield boot on an easy double-play chance gave us two unearned runs to tie the score and bring on extra innings.

Frankie Crosetti opened the tenth with a walk, and Red

Rolfe sacrificed him to second. A fumble on Charley Keller's grounder put him on first and let Crosetti go to third. I was next up and singled to right. Crosetti, of course, scored, and Keller went all the way around from first base when Goodman let the ball get away from him in the outfield. The play on Charley at the plate was close, and he banged into Lombardi, knocking the big catcher over. Fletcher waved me on to turn. I rounded third just in time to see Keller smack into Lombardi. Fletcher tried to flag me, but I had the whole play in front of me and when I saw Lombardi hit the deck I kept going and slid across the plate before Ernie could scramble to his feet and recover the ball. I knew he couldn't retrieve the ball and beat me to the plate in time.

The really alert running of the inning was Keller's. He hadn't been expected to score, but he and Fletcher took advantage of the confusion among the Cincinnati players. The runs scored by both of us were made possible by a combination of hard running and Fletcher's traffic handling: because he waved us around third, and thus we were in full stride to reach the plate.

Fans will always remember, as I will, the catch at the Yankee bull-pen gate, by the 415-foot sign, that Al Gionfriddo, substitute Dodger outfielder, made to take a three-run homer away from me in the sixth game of the 1947 World Series. The score was 9–6 in favor of the Dodgers at the time, and it probably saved the game for them.

Few seem to remember, however, that Gionfriddo's base running probably won the fourth game for the Dodgers or at least had a big share in enabling them not only to win but to rob Floyd Bevens of the honor of pitching the first no-hitter in World Series history.

With two out in the ninth, Gionfriddo was on first as a pinch runner and Pete Reiser was sent in to pinch-hit. We had a one-run lead. Gionfriddo caught us by surprise and made a clean swipe of second. This steal made Manager Bucky Harris change his entire strategy.

Harris ordered Reiser walked. This was contrary to the baseball axiom never to put the potential winning run on base. But Harris had logic behind his move. Reiser was the last left-handed pinch hitter left on the Dodger bench, and even though he had been limping the day before, he was the one remaining Dodger that the percentages said could hit a long ball and tie up the game, or hit it over the fence and win the game.

Everybody knows what happened then. Eddie Miksis was sent in to run for Reiser, and Cookie Lavagetto came up to pinch-hit for Eddie Stanky. Lavagetto, a right-handed batter, didn't figure to be as troublesome as southpaw Reiser for Bevens, a right-handed pitcher.

What Lavagetto did was to belt out the first hit of the day off Bevens, a two-bagger that scored the tying and winning runs. It was as exciting a finish as any in World Series history. It even jarred umpire Larry Goetz. As Miksis slid across with the winning score, Goetz automatically took out his whisk broom and dusted the plate, although it wouldn't be used again until the next afternoon.

Gionfriddo's base running changed the entire picture of the game. His steal of second put the tying run in scoring position, which meant pitching entirely differently to Reiser, for a single now could make the score 1 to 1. That was why Reiser was intentionally passed. But the steal was hardly noticed, even the very next day.

Floyd Bevens and I, however, will never forget Al Gionfriddo.

14: Coaching and Signs

IF YOU'RE sharp, smart, and sensible; a patient listener and a sound adviser; quick to see an advantage and ready to assume responsibility; able to make important decisions on the spot; willing to be blamed for other people's errors and to get no recognition for your own achievements; capable of directing traffic at Broadway and Forty-second Street—you, too, can be a coach.

The manager directs the attack from the bench, but once the ball is hit and the players are in motion, it's up to the coach to keep the offense moving in high gear. If he makes a mistake, it's out in the open for all the stands to see. If the play comes off perfectly, he never gets the cheer; it's all for the runner. The coach then is merely doing his job.

When Al Schacht was about to take on a coaching job for the Senators, Clark Griffith, the Washington owner, told him, "If you think you can stand the gaff of coaching at third, go to it. It's an important job, one of the most important on the ball club. It's a thankless job, and you're on the spot in every game."

The coach at first base keeps the runner going on hits to the outfield which look good for extra bases, and he watches the pitcher when the runner on first is taking his lead. He also backs up the runner on second by watching the second baseman. He usually gives the hit-and-take signs to the right-handed batters. His duties are important, but far lighter than the responsibilities of the third-base coach.

A professional coach learns quickly the importance of hand signals to base runners. Runners rarely can hear shouted in-structions above the roar of the fans, so coaches must direct them by arm and hand signals. These are simple and practically universal. Beckoning with the left hand, swinging it inward toward the chest means that the runner is to keep coming. The palms of both hands pushed out toward the runner means to hold up. Lifting the arms means that the runner needn't slide. Holding the palms down signals him to hit the dirt.

These are the signs for the base runners. The only other signals the coach gives a runner are to tell him to steal or to let him know that the hit-and-run is on. And the batter himself usually gives the hit-and-run sign, although sometimes the manager does.

Despite the fact that the coach's signs to the batter are numerous, there is no reason to make baseball signs complex. Most clubs try to keep them fairly simple, since they must be changed so frequently. Any time a player is traded to another club in the same league the signs must be changed. But they can be so simple that one club in the American League got by for years with a wink from the coach as the steal sign. It was finally abandoned when the club hired a coach who had a nervous twitch in his eyes.

While the signs themselves are simple, the coach must exercise considerable skill and ingenuity to prevent the opposition from stealing them. That is why coaches seem so jumpy on the base lines, rubbing their hands together, wiping their hands on their uniforms, fidgeting with their caps, hitching up their trousers. Only one gesture is the sign; the others are merely to confuse the opposition.

The "take" sign telling the batter not to offer at the next pitch is the most frequently used one. It may be no more than the coach's right hand touching any part of the team insignia on his uniform, the lettering across the chest, the monogram on the sleeve, or the initials on the cap. The "hit" sign, then, may be any contact between the coach's left hand and the lettering.

"Flesh-to-flesh," which is rubbing the palms together or wiping the forehead with a bare hand, is another frequently used means of signaling.

Keen eyesight is as essential to a coach as it is to a hitter. He must be able to spot the sign given by the manager on the bench and relay it to the hitter. He must also be alert to note any switch in signs by the manager. For instance, the manager flashes the bunt signal to the coach, then sees something in the defensive alignment which makes him believe that the batter may have a chance of getting a ball through the infield by hitting away.

If the batter misses a sign from the coach, the only thing for him to do is to step out of the box, adjust his uniform or knock the dirt out of his cleats with his bat, and wait for the sign to be flashed over again.

The batter gets the take sign only when the count is in his favor, such as two balls and no strikes, three and none, or three and one. He is on his own, of course, when it is three and two. When I was in my fifty-sixth-game hitting streak in 1941, Joe McCarthy played right along with me and never gave me the take sign once.

When a hit is driven to the outfield, the competent third-base coach leaves the coaching box and moves 30 or 40 feet up the line toward home plate. In this position he has an excellent view of the entire playing field, the fielders, the runners, and the ball. From here he can take full advantage of the extra-base chance that an outfield bobble or a bad throw offers.

A third-base coach who remains in the coaching box has no control over a runner after he has reached that base. If the runner makes the turn, he is past the coach and cannot be halted if it is advisable to bring him back. A third-base coach who doesn't form the habit of leaving the box and moving toward home on balls hit to the outfield doesn't remain a third-base coach very long.

Because Art Fletcher had moved up the line he was able to send Joe Gordon on home to score from first with the tying run on Babe Dahlgren's double in the opening game of the 1939 World Series. He waved Gordon to make his turn at third base, since he knew there could be no close play there, and was in position to signal him on home when he saw the throw from the outfield go to second base instead of third.

With a man on third, the coach is as busy as the flight controller at a crowded airport. He must have the runner ready to break if the ball is hit on the ground. He must hold him back if it's hit in the air. He must be sure the runner doesn't dash for the plate on just any ground ball and run headlong into an out. The runner, however, must make an initial break on all ground balls so that he can score in the event of a fumble. The coach must ensure the runner against the hazard of being doubled up on a line drive, yet have him ready to score on a pop fly if it happens to be one that an infielder has to take over his shoulder, running hard with his back to home plate and in no position to throw home in time.

In sending a runner home to score after a fly ball is caught, the coach should stand no more than a yard from him, cup his hands to his mouth, and yell "Go!" when the ball is within a few inches of the fielder's glove. The runner can't take off before the catch, but if the coach holds up his starting signal until he sees the ball land in the fielder's hands, he spots the ball valuable yardage in the race to the plate.

Coaches rarely try to steal a run on fly balls because the risk is so great, which is why fans rarely see a runner called out for leaving third before the ball is caught. Fans will notice, too, that when a runner scores from third after an outfield catch the play is seldom close. The reason is that no coach will attempt to score a runner after a fly ball unless the runner has a better than even chance of beating the throw to the plate. To judge those odds the coach must know the strength of the opposing outfielder's arm, as well as the speed of his own runner.

Judgment is a third-base coach's stock in trade. For instance, he must never send a man in from third with none out unless he is sure the runner can make it. He cannot think, "I'll send him in; it'll take a perfect play to nail him." The coach must be sure that the runner wouldn't be nailed even by a baseball miracle. With a man on third and none out, the odds that he will score eventually are so favorable that the coach cannot take any gamble whatsoever.

A coach must have the entire situation catalogued in his mind before every pitched ball. He must know the inning, the outs, the score, the speed of the runners, the throwing and fielding skill of the outfielders. He must have his strategy planned in advance, yet be prepared to improvise if a defensive lapse provides an opening.

Schacht points out that the coach's judgment can affect the whole course of a ball game.

"Take this first-inning example," he says. "Your lead-off hitter gets on base. The second batter doubles, and you try to score the lead-off man on the hit, but he is nailed at the plate, maybe by a great play and on a close decision. The third batter singles the second man home. The fourth hits into a double play, ending the inning. Now your team has one run, where it might have had two and kept the rally alive.

"One more run may not look like much in the first inning but it's like a load of wood—it gets heavier as the game goes on. Later in the game maybe your club is two runs behind instead of only one run behind. A batter reaches first, but you can't sacrifice because of the score and must run the risk of a double play. And all because the third-base coach didn't use good judgment in the first inning."

While the third-base coach must be conservative at the start of a game, he may have to take risks later in the game, depending upon the situation. If a team is one run behind, and the opposing pitcher is going well, the coach must gamble on sending in a runner, even when a good play will get him, because any scoring opportunity may be the last. When a team is a couple of runs behind, the coach can't take any chances with runners ahead of the potential tying run.

The base runners themselves pose problems for the coach. Some runners, once they get under way, can't stop themselves and will run right through the stop signs and traffic signals of the coach. Others will stop, even though the coach is frantically waving them on. There is nothing the coach can do about this, except to pretend not to hear the razzing of the fans.

There was one American League player who wouldn't leave third base after an outfield fly was caught, no matter how loud the coach yelled "Go!"

"Something just happened to him when a ball hit a glove," one of his coaches explained. "He just froze up and became stationary."

One of baseball's better third-base coaches was for a long time Mike Gonzales of the Cardinals. A Cuban, he spoke a peculiar dialect, an English-Spanish combination, but his hand signals were clear enough, except on one occasion.

At the Polo Grounds in 1937 the Cards had Henry Pippen, the pitcher, on first, Terry Moore on second, and none out. Moore and Pippen were very fast. The next man up, Art Garabaldi, hit one between the outfielders, and everybody was in motion.

Gonzales saw that Pippen could score on the hit but that Moore would have to hold up at third. With his right hand he waved Pippen to the plate; with his left he held Moore up at third. Pippen, new to the Cardinals, didn't have the hang of the Gonzales gestures and dialect. He halted halfway home, and Moore pulled up between second and third to await developments, while Gonzales screamed at them, "You go, she stay!" The developments were that the Giants tagged out both Pippen and Moore.

At the end of the inning Gonzales stalked to the dugout in a white rage.

"They no understand English," he told Manager Frank Frisch bitterly. "I tole Pippen go, and she stop; I tole Moore stop, and she go ahead. Who you do with dummies like him? I do my best, Frank; I can no do some more."

In 1931 Joe McCarthy was so embarrassed by a base-running "skull" that he never took to the coaching lines again with the Yankees, although he was in no way responsible for the lapse.

It was in a game in Washington. McCarthy was coaching at third. Lyn Lary, a smart ballplayer, was the base runner. Lou Gehrig hit a home run into the right-center bleachers so hard that the ball bounced back onto the field. Since two were out at the time, McCarthy had given Lary the sign to keep coming the instant the ball was hit.

As the ball landed in the bleachers, McCarthy clapped his hands together in appreciation of Gehrig's belt. Lary, coming toward third, was waved on, while McCarthy prepared to pat Gehrig on the back as he went by. Lary touched third and wheeled to the Yankee dugout. Gehrig jogged around the bases and thumped his foot on home plate, to be told he was out for passing the runner ahead of him. The lapse not only cost the Yankees two runs but cost Gehrig the home-run championship that season. He and Babe Ruth wound up in a tie with forty-six each.

Lary was a smart ballplayer. His turn to the dugout never

can be explained. His only excuse was that he thought the ball had been caught. But that would have made the third out, and he should have gone to his fielding position instead of to the Yankee bench.

The coach's duties on the field are only part of his work. A good, understanding coach can do much for the morale of the individual and the ball club as a whole. Most of the coaches I have known have been like Dutch uncles to the players, listening patiently to their baseball or personal problems and advising them sincerely.

A good coach frequently acts as stand-in for the manager. He invites a slumping player or a discouraged rookie to dinner and listens to his song of woe. The job of managing a ball club is extensive and intensive. The manager with coaches in whom the players can confide is spared the distraction of having players running to him with all their troubles.

The manager and his coaches work closely together. Usually a coach is a former teammate of the manager, or a retired player who worked under him. On the Pullmans, the manager usually shuts himself up in his drawing room with his coaches, to go over the plan of campaign or to rehash the game just played. On the road, the manager usually eats with the coaches. Their talk is continuously about baseball as it relates to their team.

There are men who have made a real profession of coaching, such as Art Fletcher and Mike Gonzales. Others, such as Charley Dressen, Johnny Corriden, Del Baker, Johnny Schulte, Moe Berg, Bing Miller, Benny Bengough, have proved themselves successful coaches by their long tenure of office. A coach who has been around for a long time is a good coach. Those who haven't the necessary stuff don't stay very long.

It is usually the coaches who direct all phases of practice, both pregame and spring training. During the spring, it is obviously impossible for the manager to oversee the work of his entire squad, which numbers forty or more. He parcels out the supervision among his coaches, one taking charge of the catchers, another of the outfielders, etc. At night he has long sessions with the coaches, who inform him of the showing of the various players during the day's workout.

Throughout the season the coach usually keeps a record of the pitchers who were used in batting practice the day before, in the bull pen, in other work, so that the manager knows instantly which pitchers he has available on any given day.

Coaching is hard physical work. A coach directing an infield drill to a couple of sets of infielders, or hitting "fungos" to a group of outfielders and pitchers, or catching a long session of batting practice puts in almost as much labor at his job as the ballplayers themselves and he is usually a great deal older.

The bull-pen coach is usually a former catcher. He keeps the manager advised of the sort of stuff the relief pitchers are showing in their warm-ups. In some major-league parks there is a direct telephone from bench to bull pen.

In the final game of the 1947 World Series, Johnny Schulte, Yankee bull-pen coach, advised our bench that Joe Page had plenty on his fast ball, but that his curve wasn't breaking, and that it would be good strategy to rely on his fast one to stop the Dodgers. Page went in and pitched almost perfect relief ball, but he threw only one curve. It was slammed solidly into the stands, although foul—proof enough that Schulte was right.

The one reward a coach can take away from a game is the satisfaction that he has done a tough job well.

As Al Schacht, now a New York restaurant owner, sums it up, "The best you could ever get was an even break. When I was a pitcher and somebody asked, 'How'd you do today?' I could sometimes answer, 'I won.' When I was coaching and was asked how I made out that day, the best I ever was able to say was, 'I didn't make any mistakes.' I got to dreaming about two runners winding up on the same base and a mob pouring out of the stands to chase me out of the park. One night the mob almost caught me as I scaled the center-field fence. Next day I decided to quit."

15: Slumps

THERE IS no handy cure for slumps, any more than there is a reasonable explanation for them. If anyone ever finds a slump cure, he can sit back and get rich on consultation fees, for he'll find lots of clients wherever baseball is played.

Lefty O'Doul was probably the most scientific hitter I ever knew. No one made a more detailed study of the art of hitting. This is how painstaking he was. One day, when he was my manager on the San Francisco Seals, I found him sitting on the bench, singeing the underside of his cap peak with a match.

"This is a new cap," he explained, "and I always do this to the lint of a new cap. Sometimes little threads dangle before your eyes and obscure your vision."

Yet O'Doul, who knew every trick of batting, slumped. With the Dodgers, the season after he had led the National League in batting, he went hitless in thirty-two straight times at bat. When he finally got a hit he knelt down at first base and kissed the canvas bag.

The emotional progress of a slump is approximately as follows: simple wonder, prolonged bewilderment, dawning realization, horror, grim determination, helpless rage, self-pity, relaxation, cure.

The hitter who has been getting his base knocks regularly suddenly finds his line drives dropping into the hands of a waiting fielder and his bat getting only a tiny piece of the ball or none at all. He is either hitting out in front of the ball or hitting too late. He goes hitless in a game or two and is annoyed; presently he has gone hitless in twelve times at bat and can't remember when he was on base last. A teammate says sympathetically,

"Take it easy, pal," and his condition spells itself out to him in letters a mile high—SLUMP.

Kneeling on deck, he awaits his turn at bat with all the pleasant anticipation of a small boy waiting for a licking from his dad, or a rank green rookie steeling himself to be eaten out by a bull-voiced top sergeant. And, as the rookie dreams of the day when the chevrons, or even the general's stars, are his, and the cruel sergeant cringes before him in spectacular humiliation, he grabs a bat as if it were the pitcher's windpipe and stomps to the plate, bent on hammering the aggravating baseball into a hunk of raveled yarn.

Thus he brings to the batter's box an attitude which makes it virtually impossible for him to get a hit but stamps him as lucky if he is able to get even a foul. He is pressing, which means he's overanxious, impatient, and abrupt.

In a game requiring delicate timing, coordination, and free, smooth motion, pressing is the surest means of spoiling those attributes. A slumping batter pressing for a hit is so tight that he's lucky if he can get out of the way of a close pitch.

He waggles his bat back and forth desperately, and as the pitch is delivered he's not set and is caught with the bat waving helplessly out in front of him. With the ball already streaking down from the mound he brings his bat back and tries to take his cut, all in a small fraction of a second. Thus hopelessly off balance, he must have all the breaks with him if he is to be able to connect with enough of the ball to get a weak foul, let alone a safe hit.

This is exactly what Ted Williams, a great natural hitter, did in the last two games of the 1946 World Series between the Red Sox and the Cardinals. Williams, one of the few baseball players who has batted .400 for a season, just couldn't relax.

Lefty Gomez once helped to lift a tense young player out of a slump with a wisecrack. Slumps are no respecters of persons and come to the .350 hitter and the .230 scratcher alike. This fellow was, at best, in the .230 bracket, but even for him the slump was terrible.

After striking out for the third straight time in one game he marched back to the Yankee bench in a rage, slammed his cap down on the dugout floor, and yelled, "Wow, I'm really in a slump!"

"How can you tell?" Gomez asked, dead-pan, and the kid, after a glare that should have shriveled Lefty, began to grin. He was at least on his way out of the slump. For a real, sincere grin, which must indicate some part of relaxation, is about as effective a way of shaking off a slump as any other.

Almost any way out of a slump is *about as effective* as any other, for there is no pat cure. Ty Cobb, who wasn't immune to slumps despite his record for the greatest number of hits in the history of the game, had a home remedy which he would use whenever he ran into a long no-hit spell. Just as everyone who has his own remedy for the common cold, Cobb had great faith in his slump cure; in fact, he never revealed it while he was an active player.

"I wouldn't even swing at the ball," Cobb now explains. "I'd just stand up at the plate and slap it right back at the pitcher—try to hit it directly into his hands, as a matter of fact. Somehow just meeting the ball that way would give me confidence, and the next time up I'd be as natural at the plate as I ever was."

Ballplayers who are fast runners sometimes can bunt their way out of slumps. John McGraw was a great believer in this slump cure and once fined his great outfield star, the late Ross Youngs, for not bunting when he was in a slump.

"With your speed you're almost a cinch to beat out a bunt," he told Youngs, "and if you get on base, it's a hit. It helps you and it helps the club."

This method lifted Dusty Cooke out of one of the greatest

opening-of-the-season slumps on record. When Cooke, a rookie with wonderful prospects, came up to the Yankees, he went through the entire first month of the season without a hit. In the middle of May one of the Yankee veterans recommended the bunt treatment. Next time up Cooke managed to drag the ball down the first-base line, beat it to the bag, and soon was out of his slump.

Even a dinky hit is a tremendous restorer of confidence, and loss of confidence is one of the chief reasons why a slump-bound player tightens up, why he presses.

Hitters noted for their keen eye suddenly begin to slap at bad pitches, no longer trusting their judgment and becoming afraid to "take" these tosses lest they be called out on strikes. Even worse, they "take" pitches that are right down their alley, and are called out on strikes on pitches that ordinarily they could hit a mile.

Almost as if to prove the superstition that bad things come in threes, it is inevitable that a hitter in a slump loses not only his skill and his confidence but also his luck at the plate. The few balls he manages to hit solidly travel on a string into the hands of a fielder. When he's on a hitting streak, just the reverse is true. Pop flies off the handle of his bat drop in safely for Texas leaguers. Balls topped so badly that he has almost missed them completely dribble through the infield so slowly that he can reach first almost in a walk. In a slump he never gets a break like that. Everything goes wrong.

Some players recommend extra batting practice—a lot of it —as a slump cure. They get out to the park early and get some-one to pitch to them for an hour or more; somewhere along in these protracted practice sessions the swing may slip back into the groove and the bat begin to meet the ball solidly again.

When Babe Herman, a consistent .300 hitter, was with

Brooklyn, he had a milkman meet him in the morning at Ebbets Field and pitch to him. The milkman, Bill Boylan, had wonderful control, the primary quality of a batting-practice pitcher; in fact the Dodgers took him along on this assignment on their last Western swing in 1947.

A batter in a slump becomes such an object of pity that every friend and well-wisher tries to help him—with advice. They will tell him not to press, to relax, to take a shorter stride, a longer stride, to open his stance, to close it. They may even tell him exactly what he's doing wrong, and how to correct it. He may even tell himself. But to correct it is a tougher matter. Sometimes a player can't recognize a fault even when it's proved to him.

Near the end of the 1940 season, after several leading golfers had recommended studying movies of their swings as a means of correcting flaws, Larry MacPhail, then president of the Dodgers, undertook an experiment with films as a possible aid to hitters. He had movies made of his players at bat.

Pete Coscarart, a right-handed hitter, had developed a fault while the film was being made. Just as he started to swing he dipped his head toward his left shoulder. He wasn't plate-shy; he had just picked up this flaw somewhere. Obviously it meant that he was taking his eye off the ball.

When the Dodgers gathered for spring training at Havana the next year, Coscarart still had the same flaw. Manager Leo Durocher, the coaches, and other players told Pete he was dipping his head and taking his eye off the ball. He denied it. They ran off the film for him.

"I don't care how it looks in the pictures; I know I'm not ducking into the pitch," Coscarart insisted. That is typical of a hitter in a slump.

The first thing he'll do when he realizes he's in a slump is to run up to the bench and ask everyone in sight, "What am I doing wrong?" They'll tell him, and he'll go right up to the plate and do the same thing all over again.

Sometimes, however, a player learns about a mechanical fault and is able to correct it. My wife once helped me break a slump by a chance remark.

At the Yankee Stadium she had the same seat for every game, just to the right of home plate. As a right-handed hitter, I stand, of course, at the left of the plate. When I finished a swing with a good follow-through, my back was turned squarely to her.

On the way home from a game after I'd gone a week with no luck at the plate, my wife said, "You know, I can't see the Number 5 on the back of your uniform any more." I asked what she was talking about, and she explained that usually, at the end of my follow-through, the number on my back was turned to her but now it didn't show.

It was a perfect tip-off to me that I was overstriding, getting my feet too wide apart, with the result that I couldn't pivot freely. I went back to my normal shorter step forward and began to hit again.

Slumps affect entire ball clubs as well as individuals. But while sometimes an individual slump is possibly explained on the grounds of personal worries, what is the possible explanation for a mass slump? I've seen clubs floundering in slumps as helplessly as any individual player. I don't mean just losing streaks, but stretches in which a club is shut out a couple of times in one week and is held to less than a half-dozen hits for four games out of five.

Some managers try to meet that condition by telling all the players on the club to take a night off and forget their troubles. When Bill Terry succeeded John McGraw as manager of the Giants he abolished the check-in conducted each midnight by the trainer because he thought McGraw had been too strict. It wasn't long before Terry reinstalled the curfew and was as stiff a disciplinarian as McGraw had been.

In 1937 the Giants went into a terrific slump on a Western trip. It looked as if they would blow the pennant. Terry was desperate. He told his players that for that night, and that night only, there would be no curfew. They could return to their hotel rooms (they were in Cincinnati) whenever they pleased. One of the newspapermen traveling with the club heard about it and decided to sit up in the hotel lobby and check the boys in, just to see how twenty-five ballplayers would react to the sudden lifting of the curfew. He checked in the last man at about a half hour after midnight. They had become so used to the curfew that they couldn't stay awake! Presently they woke out of their slump (just as they had slipped into it—for no apparent reason) and went on to win the pennant.

I've seen ballplayers get out to the park early for extra batting practice in an effort to break a slump and I've seen some ballplayers pass up batting practice altogether, just to see what they could do if they hit "cold." Neither system can be recommended as a cure. The slump just runs its course. It's like that old story about the city slicker who drove up to the country filling station in a terrible downpour and asked the attendant if he thought it would ever stop raining.

"Well," said the country boy, eying the sky thoughtfully, "it always has."

And that's the way it is with slumps.

There is, I think, a difference between a slump and what ball players call a "bad year." A bad year is a succession of slumps, with scarcely any breathing spells in between. Any one of a number of things can cause a bad year; all add up to some persistently nagging worry that keeps the batter from putting his mind entirely on the job at hand.

The difference between a slump and a bad year is that a

slump, provided it is not too protracted, is usually followed by a spurt in which the batter hits far above his usual average, so that he evens off when figured in terms of the full season.

Ballplayers, being human, rarely think in terms of the full season. A batter who hits .290 says, "I would have hit .300 easy if it hadn't been for that slump in July." He forgets all about the rash of base hits he broke out with in August, which was as far above his normal pace as July was below it.

If a ballplayer in a slump could console himself with the thought that once out of it he'll probably hit like a house afire, it would help his frame of mind, but I've never met a ballplayer who could reason that way. There's always the horrible thought that maybe this is the end, that the pitchers are on to you at last, that you're all washed up. It is not a frame of mind which lends itself readily to consolation.

Ballplayers in a batting slump are not pleasant companions. Baseball wives, baseball families, close friends—all are in for it when a player is in a slump. Rubbed raw by repeated failures that seem destined never to halt, he blows up as quickly as a penny firecracker. The best-intended advice he may have begged for may be just the extra irritation that makes him explode. At times like this, the fellow is best left alone.

There was an old story about Jay Kirke and his wife, a lady who knew her baseball. When Kirke would return from the ball park, she would greet him with the following little ditty.

> Well, my honey, well, my Jay,
> How many hits did you get today?

Since Jay murdered pitching in the minors, he usually had a glowing report to make, listing his singles and his extra-base hits. But a slump came to Jay, even as it comes to the rest of us. For a couple of days running he had no feats to report, no hits at all, in fact. When Mrs. Kirke greeted him with the jingle on the third day, Jay burst out, "Look, you do the cooking for this family and I'll do the hitting."

A batter who is not hitting will attempt fantastic remedies, just as a pitcher with a lame arm will submit to the ministrations of any quack. The late Herb Pennock, certainly one of the most intelligent players the game ever produced, as well as one of the greatest southpaw pitchers, once let bees sting his ailing left arm on the theory of an amateur doctor who told him that bee venom would revitalize it.

It didn't, of course, but the quack was around a few days later telling Pennock the reason the remedy wasn't effective was that he used domesticated bees; wild bees would positively do the trick.

"You know," said Pennock, later general manager of the Phillies, "I was so desperate that I considered going out to the woods and looking for wild bees!"

Changing bats is a favorite resort of slumping hitters. One of the most famous hits of all baseball history, the hit which broke up the famous 1908 game between the Cubs and Giants in which Fred Merkle failed to touch second, was made with a borrowed bat. Al Bridwell, Giant shortstop, made the single which scored what was seemingly the winning run in this game with a bat belonging to Buck Herzog. Herzog was hitting well, and Bridwell had been in a slump, so he figured maybe Buck's bat would be lucky.

There is no telling when a slump will overtake a hitter. I fell into one of the worst of my career in the spring of 1947 when I was leading the American League in batting. Everything I hit had been dropping safely for me, and all of a sudden I found myself pushing at the ball. I not only wasn't getting any hits but I wasn't even hitting the ball hard. There was no earthly reason for me to start pressing at this particular time, but there it was.

About the only advice you can give a slumping ballplayer is to tell him to keep swinging. As long as he is swinging he has a chance of eventually getting a hit. Perhaps the best cure is a day or two on the bench, but I've met few ballplayers who would volunteer to be taken out of the line-up during a slump. Depressed as he is by his slump, there's always the fear in his mind that he may never get back in again.

Brooklyn, back in the middle 1930's, bought an outfielder from Memphis in the Southern Association who had a fine record as a minor-league slugger. But he introduced himself to the majors with an unshakable slump. The Dodgers, in sixth place that season, kept him in the line-up every day, but he just couldn't get a hit. At last he said to Otto Miller, a Dodger coach, "You know what it is? It's those pitchers. They keep throwing me curves all the time. They don't want me to hit!"

"That," Miller answered, "is the general idea."

Fresco Thompson, field director for the Brooklyn organization, was given charge of a group of boys in a teen-age tournament in the summer of 1947. A youngster on the squad was having slump trouble.

"I wish you'd watch me and advise me, Mr. Thompson," the boy requested. "I'm cutting just a trifle under the ball all the time and I'd like to know what I can do about it."

"How far are you cutting under the ball, son?" asked Thompson.

"Just about this much," answered the boy, holding his thumb and forefinger about a quarter of an inch apart.

"O.K., son," the old professional said. "Tomorrow we'll just go to the shoemaker and get you a pair of inner soles."

How to Score

by RED BARBER

Sports Director, Columbia Broadcasting System
World Series Broadcaster

SCORING A BALL GAME can be as simple or as complex as the fan wishes to make it. I've known fellow broadcasters who keep scorebooks as detailed as a researcher's calculations on atomic energy, and I've friends who content themselves with merely marking a large "O" on their score sheet when a batter is retired, a large "X" if he makes a hit, a "W" if he gets a base on balls, and an "E" if he reaches base on an error.

I doubt if there are any two people, fans, writers, or broadcasters, who keep score with identical symbols and systems. I do know that any fan who acquires the habit of scoring his own ball games will find that it adds much to his enjoyment of the pastime. The only important thing about keeping score is that the scorer himself must be able to read his scorecard back, a week or a year later. If it is intelligible to him, it doesn't matter what system he employs.

The first fundamental of keeping score is to number players according to their defensive positions. The accepted system is to start with the pitcher as No. 1, and the catcher, No. 2; then swing around the infield, with first base, No. 3; second base, No. 4; third base, No. 5; list the shortstop as No. 6 and pick up the left fielder as No. 7; the center fielder, No. 8; and the right fielder, No. 9.

There are, of course, several variations of this, some scorers preferring to label the shortstop No. 5 and the third baseman No. 6. Others number the right fielder No. 7 and the left fielder No. 9, but the system just outlined is most widely used.

Once you have your fielding positions numbered, you are ready to begin scoring. On any scorecard, beside each batter's name, are nine squares, one for each inning. Each square is blank or is divided, a diamond placed in its middle, leaving a small triangle in each corner.

Whatever type of scorecard or book you use, all you need to remember is that you trace the batter's progress around the square precisely as he advances around the infield, beginning with the lower left as home.

Let's keep score for an inning, one in which six men come to bat. Say it's the first inning, and they're the first six men in the batting order. Here they are:

> Smith
> Green
> Black
> Jones
> Brown
> Johnson

Smith, the lead-off hitter, draws a base on balls. Mark a "W," "B," or even "BB" in the lower right corner of the first-inning square beside his name.

Green hits one to the shortstop, who throws to the second baseman to force Smith. Put "6-4" in the upper right corner of Smith's square, showing exactly how he was retired at second base, shortstop to second baseman. Put down "FO" in the lower right corner of Green's square, which means he reached first on a force-out.

Green steals second. Write "SB" in the upper right corner of his box, which tells plainly how he got to second. Had he been out on a throw from the catcher you would have written "2-4" or "2-6," depending on whether second baseman or shortstop took the throw for the put-out.

Let's complicate it a bit. The shortstop fumbles one to let

Black reach first. Mark "E-6" in Black's lower right corner. "E" means he got on first by an error, "6" means the error was by the shortstop. You may even want to classify errors precisely, using "E" for a fumbled grounder, "W" for a wild throw, or "M" for a muffed fly.

HOW TO SCORE.

		1	2	3
SMITH	2B.	64 W		
GREEN	3B.	3 SB 4 FO		
BLACK	CF.	5 E6		
JONES	1B.	8		
BROWN	LF.	XC		
JOHNSON	SS.	K		

On the shortstop's error on Black, Green goes to third. Note his progress by putting a "3" in the upper left corner of his square which shows that he moved up as a result of whatever happened to the third man in the line-up.

Jones, batting fourth, drives a long fly to the center fielder, and Green scores from third after the catch. Green now has traveled all around the infield, and, on the score card, all around the square. In the lower left corner enter a four, because he was brought home by the fourth man in the line-up.

Brown, next up, singles, and you note it with a small "x" in the lower right corner of his square. If you're a fiend for detail, you can make it "sc," "xr," or "xl," thus noting whether he singled to center, right, or left.

Black, who was on first, moved up to second on the hit, so put a "5" in the second-base corner of his square, showing that he was advanced by the doings of the hitter in the number five slot. If Black is a heady runner and goes all the way to third, put a "5" in that corner too.

Johnson strikes out to end the inning, and wins a large "K" in the lower right-hand corner of his square. For complete details, you may use "KO" if he went down swinging, "KC" if he was called out on strikes, "KF" if he was declared out because he bunted foul on third strike, or "K-3" if the catcher dropped the third strike and had to throw him out at first base.

Since an "x" in the first corner indicates a single, "x" in the first two corners means a two-bagger, "x" in the first three is a triple, and "x" in all four corners is a home run.

When numbers for fielding positions appear in the corners in combination with other fielders' numbers, the man who makes the assist is entered first, and the player who makes the put-out, second. For instance, when the first baseman (3) takes a throw from the shortstop (6) to make the put-out, the play is entered "6-3." If it's a double play from second baseman to shortstop to first baseman, it's "4-6-3." If the batter grounds to the first baseman, who fields the ball and steps on the bag to make the put-out unassisted, it's "3-U."

"WP" is simple and sufficient for a wild pitch, and "PB" for a passed ball, but symbols may be carried out to almost any degree of detail the scorekeeper wishes. Although the fielder's number in the lower right corner is enough to show that the batter flied out, and to whom, some scorers want to know just what type of fly ball he hit. The use "P-6" for a pop to the shortstop, "F-2" for a foul to the catcher, and "L-9" for a line drive to the right fielder.

There was a time when it was difficult for a fan scoring a game to keep an accurate box score because he had no way of knowing whether a close play was ruled a hit or an error. Now, however, there is a light or a sign on the scoreboard in almost every park to tell the fans the official scorer's decision.

My advice to any fan who wants to keep score is to start with a simple, elementary system and then add his own embellishments as he goes along. You can grow more meticulous as you become more experienced; noting, for instance, an intentional pass as "PW" to distinguish it from an unintended walk, which is listed without adornments as just "W."

Henry McLemore, the columnist, tells of the scoring system which his wife Jean devised for the 1938 World Series between the Yankees and the Cardinals. She even worked out her own score sheets, which were about a foot square. When a Cub pitcher intentionally walked Joe Gordon, Mrs. McLemore carefully noted down "HDWH."

"What's that mean?" Henry asked his wife.

"It means," she replied, " 'He Deliberately Walked Him.' "

As I said at the start, the only important thing about scoring is for you to be able to understand your own system.

Index

A

Alabama State League, 29
Amateur baseball, 1
  aptitudes for, 14
  bad habits in, 9
  change of position in, 12-13, 15
  choice of position in, 12, 15
  dangers of, 8-9
  development of, 6-8
  need for adapting for young boys,
    8
  need for supervision of, 8, 10-11
  rules for, 11, 15
  scouting of, 15
  ways of learning, 17-27
American Association, 30, 37, 178
American League, 17, 89, 97, 117,
  138, 146, 152, 165, 184, 189, 203
  (*See also* names of clubs in)
American League Junior Baseball,
  number of players in, 1
  teams playing in, 1
American Legion Junior Baseball, 17
Arizona-Texas League, 29
Arm, strained, 9, 164-165
  strong, 15, 39, 98, 100
  (*See also* Pitchers)
Athletics (club) (*see* Philadelphia
  Athletics)
Athletics, organized, 1
  and personal freedom, 18
  unorganized, 18
Attendance, total, in 1947, for pro-
  fessional-league games, 1

B

Bad year, definition of, 201
Bag, bluffing at, 79
  covering the, 78
  on steals, 81
  in double play, 61-62
  and first baseman, 56-63
  playing off the, 57-60
  tagging the, 55
Baker, Del, 161, 191
Baker Bowl, 161
Balks, 95, 166-167, 179
Balls, butterfly, fingering for, 158
  curve, 40, 74, 115, 120, 131, 157
    fingering for, 156
    sign for, 122
  description of, 139
  fast, 40, 74, 119-120, 131, 154
    sign for, 122
    timing of, 139n.
  fly, 106, 124, 135, 187-188
    how to field, 100
    in "one old cat," 7
    turning of, into put-outs, 116,
      124
  fork, 158
  foul, 62, 106, 116, 185-186
  ground, 89, 102, 105
    how to field, 99-100, 108
  low, 113-114
  palm, 161
  quality of, 8, 125
  slow, fingering for, 157-158
Baltimore, 13, 49
Bancroft, Dave, 108-109
Barber, Red, 205
Barrow, Ed, 13
Base runners, bluffing by, 78
  and coaches, 189-190
  in double play, 60, 70-71, 102, 173,
    177-180
  and hidden-ball play, 94-95, 174
    precaution against, 94-95
  instructions for, 171-172, 175
  in offensive plays, 179-180
  picked off third, 93-94
  qualifications for, 170-171

Base runners, (*continued*)
  in relation to first baseman, 62-63
  in relation to pitcher, 174, 179
  in sacrifice plays, 92
  safe at second, 72, 122
  signals to, 184, 187-188
  sliding by, 82, 172, 175-177
  in steals, 104-105, 119-120, 174-179
    bluff, 176
    double, 177-178
    home, 178-179
    trapped off base, 64, 107
    (*See also* Base running)
Base running, 170-182
  for extra bases, 174-175
  recklessness of, 179
  for stolen bases, 174
Baseball law, 50
Baseball schools, instruction in, 25
  location of, 25
  private, tuition in, 25
  run by clubs, Dodgers, 25-26
    Giants, 26
    invitational, 25-26
    noninvitational, 26
    Washington Senators, 26
  scouting in, 25
Baseball writers, 60, 67, 141
Bases, empty, 87
  filled, 88, 91
  first, 10, 53, 172-174
  location of, 8
  in "one old cat," 7
  second, 9-10, 53, 172-174
    and shortstop, 63
  stolen, 104, 119, 174-179
  third, 53, 172-174, 177-178, 186-189
  unprotected, 87-88
  (*See also* Base runners)
Basinski, Eddie, 74
Basket catch, 100
Bat, 139, 141-142
Batters, 17-18, 22
  ability of, to hit bunts, 147-149
    to judge pitches, 147
  attributes of, 140-141
  choke, 143, 149-150

crosshanded, 143
  in double plays, 69
  grip for, 142-143, 150
  left-handed, 75, 78, 113-114, 131,
    149-150
  long ball, 143
  in major leagues, 43, 115
    rookie, 47
  in minor leagues, 43
  mission of, 139-140
  natural, 49
  in "one old cat," 7, 9
  outfielders as, 125
  and pitcher, 139, 151-153, 161-164
    distance between, 139
  plate-shyness of, 150-151
  position of, in box, 142
  requirements for, 140-141
  right-handed, 78, 94, 108, 113, 131,
    149-150, 157, 182
  scientific, 194
  types of, 76-77
  weapon of, 139
Batters' box, 139, 142
Batting averages, .220, 43, 140
  .300, 198
  .330, 140
  .400, 67, 195
Beazley, Johnny, 104, 162
Bengough, Benny, 191
Bennett, George, 19
Berg, Moe, 14, 191
Berger, Wally, 180
Bevans, Floyd, 181-182
Big Four, 110-111
Big leagues (*see* Major leagues)
Blackwell, Ewell, 164
Bluege, Ossie, 26
Bohne, Sammy, 95
Bonuses, for major-league players, 24
  outlawing of, 24
Bordagaray, Frenchy, 167
Boston, 14
Boston Braves, 14, 40, 44-45, 49, 71,
  83, 117-118, 173-174
Boston Red Sox, 13, 26, 47, 49, 51, 98,
  130, 133, 166, 195

Boudreau, Lou, 71, 97, 102
Boudreau shift, 151-152
Boylan, Bill, 199
Boys Club leagues, 1
  of San Francisco, 17, 20
Bragan, Bobbie, 14
Braves (see Boston Braves)
Bridwell, Al, 203
Broadcasters, sports, 60, 205
Brooklyn, 14, 23
Brooklyn Dodgers, 27, 40, 44, 49, 51,
  66, 71, 74, 86, 89, 91, 95-96, 114,
  118-119, 122-123, 152-153, 155,
  161-162, 167, 170, 173, 181-182,
  192, 194, 199, 204
  baseball school of, 26-27
  and Jackie Robinson, 50-51
Brown, Jimmy, 104
Browns (see St. Louis Browns)
Bunts, 103, 119, 168
  as cure for slumps, 196-197
  down base line, 64-66
  fielded by catcher, 120
  hit by batters, 147-149
  with man on first, 63
  with men on second and third, 63
  by pitcher, 62-63
  sacrifice, 53, 91-92, 149
    defense against, 91-92
  situations demanding, 91
  skill at placing, 149
  surprise, 62, 78
  swinging, 84, 89
  turning of, into force-out at third,
    63
Bushwicks, 21
Business side of baseball, 50-51
Butterfly ball (see Balls)

C

Camilli, Dolph, 57, 66, 86
Canadian-American League, 29
Careers in baseball, encouragement
  for, 26
  odds against, 16
  other than as player, 37-38

rules for, 19
  special abilities for, 15
Carey, Max, 174
Casey, Hugh, 86, 114-115, 152, 162-
  163, 165
Catch, diving or shoestring, 129-130
Catchers, amateur, 13-14
  bluffing by, 117-119
  correct stance for, 111-112, 120-121
  difficulties of, 13, 110
  and double steal, 117
  duties of, 110-120
  extra-step habit of, 9-10
  fielding bunts, 120
  footwork of, 113
  and foul flies, 116
  and hitters, 112-113
  injuries to, 113
  and mask, 110, 115-117
  and missed balls, 113-114
  physical requirements of, 110-111,
    120
  and pitch-outs, 119
  professional, 13-14, 39
    advancement of, 40
  in relation to batter, 115-116, 119-
    120
    to pitcher, 112-115, 119, 121
  rules for, 116-117, 120
  signalling by, 74, 111, 115, 120-122,
    168
  as team strategist, 115
  and third base, 77, 94
  (See also Catching)
Catching, art of, 110-123
  two-handed vs. one-handed, 130
Change of position, among amateurs,
  12-13
  among professionals, 13-14
  if right-handed, 15
Charley horse, 19
  definition of, 45
  precautions against, 45-46
Chase, Hal, 57
Chattanooga, Senators' farm club at,
  26-27
Chicago, 5, 14, 20, 52

Chicago Cubs, 5, 37, 66, 71, 82, 119, 122-123, 167, 203, 209
Chicago White Sox, 5, 14, 18, 138, 143, 165
Cincinnati, 14, 33, 49, 82, 95, 164, 180-181
Cleveland Indians, 2, 52, 71, 83, 97, 133, 151, 153, 167
Coaches, 13, 61, 94, 106
  bull-pen, 192
  experienced, 191
  first-base, 172, 183
  and fly balls, 187-188
  judgment needed by, 188-189
  major-league, 38
  as morale builders, 191
  and offensive plays, 183
  pitches stolen by, 161
  during practice and training, 191-192
  in relation to managers, 183, 186, 191-192
  requirements for, 183, 186
  rewards of, 192
  screening signals from, 111
  signals by, 172, 183-187
  signs stolen by, 151
  strategy of, 188-189
  third-base, 172, 180, 183, 186-190
  (See also Coaching)
Coaching, 183-193
  difficulties of, 192
  as profession, 38, 191
  thanklessness of, 183
Cobb, Ty, 5, 142, 196
Cochrane, Mickey, 110
College baseball, 1
Combs, Earl, 128
Competitive attempts at baseball, first, 6-7
Control, in pitching, 39
Cooke, Dusty, 130, 196, 198
Cooney, Johnny, 14
Cooper, Mort, 13-14, 122
Cooper, Walker, 13-14, 104
Corriden, Johnny, 191
Coscarart, Pete, 199

Cotton States League, 29
Cronin, Joe, 98
Crosetti, Frank, 97, 101, 180-181
Cubs (see Chicago Cubs)
Cunny-thumbing, 164
Curfew, 200-201
Curve ball (see Balls)
Cuyler, Kiki, 82

D

Dahlgren, Babe, 57, 180, 187
Danning, Harry, 10
Davis, Harry, 57
"Dead Pan" (see DiMaggio, Joe)
Dean, Dizzy, 102, 138, 169
DeBerry, Hank, 168, 173
Defense, over-shifted, 151-152, 179
  pressure on, 171, 180
Derringer, Paul, 180
Detroit, 98
Detroit Tigers, 24, 40, 62, 71, 76, 83, 102, 132
Diamonds, municipal, 2
  size of, for boys under sixteen, 8
    regulation, 8
  softball, 8
Dickey, Bill, 76, 104, 110, 112-113, 132, 147
DiMaggio, Dominic, 23, 141
DiMaggio, Joe, in American League, 89
  anecdotes about, 20, 132, 200
  bats used by, 142
    grip for, 143
  in Boys Club League, 17
  first baseball pay earned by, 20
  first competitive playing by, 7
  first professional game of, 13
  hitting streak of, 84, 186
  length of stride of, 145
  minor-league experience of, 31, 42-43
  in 1937-38 World Series, 10
  in 1939 World Series, 181
  in 1947 World Series, 152, 162-163, 181-182

outfield technique of, 126, 128
as rookie, 44
with San Francisco Seals, 42-43, 153, 194
in slump, 200, 203
DiMaggio, Mrs. Joe, 200
DiMaggio, Joe, Jr., 110
Dodgers (*see* Brooklyn Dodgers)
Double-headers, 32, 52
night, 32
Double plays (*see* Plays)
Draft, eligibility for, 36
and farm system, 38-39, 50
judgment of, 37
purpose of, 36
Draft price, variation in, 36
Drag, definition of, 149
Dressen, Charley, 82, 161, 191
"Ducky Wucky" (*see* Medwick, Joe)
Dunne, Bert V., 8
Durocher, Leo, 89, 91, 199
Dusters, 58, 94, 121, 150
Dykes, Jimmy, 143

E

Eastern League, 30, 32
Eastern Shore League, 29
Eating, moderation in, 19
regularity in, 19
Ebbets Field, 27, 114, 127, 167, 173
Edwards, Bruce, 23
Elliott, Bob, 83
Elliott, Rowdy, 119
Engel, Joe, 26
Etten, Nick, 20

F

Fadeaway (*see* Screwball)
Fans, abuse and applause by, 137-138
curiosity of, 2-3
devotion of, 3
difference between players and, 5
loyalty of, 5
and outfielders, 137
participation of, 1-6
and scoring, 205
similarity of, to players, 2-3
Farm clubs, 22, 26-27
Farm system, 26-27
growth of, 38
handicaps of, 38
injustices of, 38
operation of, 38-39
as source of potential big-league players, 38
Fast ball (*see* Balls)
Feller, Bob, 27, 139*n*., 162, 167-168
Fenway Park, 136
Fewster, Chick, 173-174
Fielders, 2, 17
center, 128, 131, 135
first baseman as, 53-54, 56, 60-61, 67
left, 93, 131
relays to, 74
right, 74-75, 113
second baseman as, 68-75
shortstops as, 98-109
(*See also* Infielders; Outfielders)
Fifth infielder (*see* Pitchers)
Fingering, 155-158
First baseman, 7, 36, 44-45
ability of, to make pickups, 55
to stretch, 55-56
agility of, 56-57
cooperation with pitcher, 59-60, 66-67, 93, 168
in double play, 60-61
duties of, 66
at bat, 67
examples of, 106
fielding by, 60-61, 67
left-handed, 53-54, 56, 63
right-handed, 53, 56
gloves for, 62
in hit-and-run play, 65
importance of position play to, 62
left-handed, 14-15, 53, 55, 58
need of judgment by, 57-58, 61-62, 65
off-the-bag play by, 57-60, 63
in play bunted down the line, 65-66

First baseman (*continued*)
  and pop flies, 87
  prescription for, 53, 55-56
  purpose of holding man on base, 64
  in relation to runners, 62-63
  right-handed, 54
  top-notch, value of, 55
  (*See also* Bases)
Firte, Lou, 40
Fitzsimmons, Freddie, 110-111, 155, 158, 169
Fletcher, Art, 161, 180-181, 187, 191
Florida, baseball schools in, 25
Fly ball (*see* Balls)
Follow-through, in pitching, 166
Fordham University, 143
Fothergill, Fatty, 138
Foul ball (*see* Balls)
Foul line, 172
Fox, Pete, 132
French, Larry, 155, 167
Frisch, Frankie, 83, 143, 190

G

Galan, Augie, 13
Games, All-Star, 147
  competition, 46-47
  exhibition, 33, 46, 138, 161
  night (*see* Night games)
  practice, 46
  (*See also* World Series)
Garabaldi, Art, 189
Gautreau, Doc, 174
Gehrig, Lou, 49, 59, 67, 180, 190
Gehringer, Charley, 71, 76-77, 132
Georgia Peach (*see* Cobb, Ty)
Gionfriddo, Al, 181-182
Goetz, Larry, 182
Gomez, Lefty, 76, 108, 146-147, 195
Gonzales, Mike, 161, 189-191
Goodman, Ival, 181
Gordon, Joe, 71, 76, 102, 104, 180, 187, 209
Gowdy, Hank, 116
Greenberg, Hank, 62
Griffith, Clark, 183
Griffith, Tommy, 119

Grimes, Burleigh, 161
Grimm, Charley, 58
Grove, Lefty, 162
Guess hitters, 151

H

Harris, Bucky (Stanley), 26, 47, 182
Hartung, Clint, 154
Hazing, elimination of, 47
Henrich, Tommy, 113-114, 127, 136, 153, 171
Herman, Babe, 173-174, 198-199
Herman, Billy, 71, 86, 122
Herzog, Buck, 203
Hidden-ball play (*see* Plays)
High school baseball, 1
Hit-and-run (*see* Plays)
Hits, base, 148
  bunting for, 149
  behind the runner, 78
  extra-base, 75
  fly, 75
  pop-up, 87, 149
  (*See also* Balls; Plays)
Hitters (*see* Batters)
Hitting, 139-153
  elements controlled by batter, 141
  overstriding in, 145-146
  right-handed, proper swing in, 143-145
  stance for, 142-143
  (*See also* Batters)
Hogan, Shanty, 32, 111
Home plate, 8-9, 53, 63, 66, 120-121, 171
  in relation to pitcher, 154-155
  size of, 139
  stealing (*see* Base runners; Bases; Steals)
Home runs, 67, 129, 181
  introduction of, 149
Hornsby, Rogers, 25, 74, 108, 141
Hot Springs, Arkansas, baseball school at, 25
Hubbell, Carl, 40, 110-111, 138, 153, 157, 169

Huggins, Miller, 40
Hurst, Tim, 52

I

Indians (*see* Cleveland Indians)
Infield, 12, 68
Infielders, 13-14, 55-56, 58
  advancement of, 40
  in double steal, 79-92
  and first basemen, 58-59
  and line drives, 100
  and relay throws, 133
  and second basemen, 77-78
  (*See also* Fielders)
International League, 30
Interstate League, 30

J

Jackson, Travis, 5-6
Johnson, Bill, 76
Johnson, Walter, 162
Joost, Eddie, 97
Jorgensen, Spider, 23, 44
Judge, Joe, 57, 61

K

Kampouris, Alec, 82
Kansas City, 13
Keeler, Willie, 150
Kell, George, 83
Keller, Charley, 181
Kelly, Long George, 66, 106
Keltner, Ken, 83, 85
Kieran, John, 67, 141
Kirke, Jay, 146-147, 202-203
Kitty League, 29
Knucklers, 120, 155
  fingering for, 158
Kuhel, Joe, 26, 57
Kurowski, Whitey, 162

L

Lary, Lyn, 190-191
Lavagetto, Cookie, 182

Lazzeri, Tony, 76
Leagues, major (*see* Major leagues)
  minor (*see* Minor leagues)
  organized, advantages of playing
    in, 17-18
    Junior American Legion, 17
    number of professionals devel-
      oped from, 17
    scholastic, 17
    Sunday-school, 17
Leonard, Dutch, 120
Lewis, Buddy, 26
Lighting systems, 28, 33-34
  improvement in, 33
Line drives, how to catch, 100
Lit Brothers team, 21
Little Rock Travelers, 5
Lobert, Hans, 14
Logan Squares, 21
Lombardi, Ernie, 82, 143, 181
Lone Star League, 29
Longhorn League, 29
Lopez, Al, 49
Louisville, 37, 146, 178
Luque, Adolfo, 169
Lyons, Ted, 165

M

McCarthy, Joe, 6, 16, 23, 37, 47, 83,
  98, 101, 122-123, 132, 146-147, 163,
  186, 190
McCormick, Frank, 27
McGraw, John, 108-109, 118, 133,
  146, 162, 196, 200
Mack, Connie, 128, 146
McLemore, Henry, 209
MacPhail, Larry, 33, 199
McQuinn, George, 49
Mails, Walter "Duster," 153
Major leagues, 13-14, 16, 24-25, 34, 36
  barnstorming by, 21-22
  compared with minor leagues, 42
  competition for places in, 42
  life in, 28, 51
  number playing in, 16, 28
  outfielders in, 124-126, 132-133

Major leagues (*continued*)
  shortstops in, 105
  total attendance at games of, in
    1947, 1
  transportation for, 51-52
  (*See also* names of leagues and
    clubs in)
Managers, 13, 108-109, 132, 161, 167-
    169, 178, 182, 190
  of amateur-league teams, 18
  career as, 37
  desire to impress, 48
  gambles of, 91
  of major-league teams, 46, 191
    (*See also* names of managers)
  and mass slumps, 200-201
  of minor-league teams, 32, 194
  in relation to coaches, 183, 186,
    191-192
Mancuso, Gus, 110-111
Mann, Leslie, 117-118
Maranville, Rabbit, 100, 123
Marion, Marty, 97, 102, 104
Martin, Pepper, 119, 175
Mathewson, Christy, 4, 157
Meany, Tom, 173
Medwick, Joe "Muscles," 6, 147
Memphis, 204
Merkle, Fred, 203
Meusel, Irish, 132
Meyer, Billy, 115, 178-179
Miksis, Eddie, 182
Miller, Bing, 191
Miller, Eddie, 49, 74
Miller, Otto, 204
Minor leagues, 10, 14, 22, 24
  advancement in, 35-36
  age of players in, 34
  apprenticeship in, 27-30
    necessary speed of, 35
  classifications of, Class A, 21, 41
    living conditions in, 37
    salaries in, 30, 37
    Class AA, salaries in, 30
    Class AAA, 30, 35-36, 38, 43
    salaries in, 30
    Class B, 21, 36, 40

    salaries in, 30
    Class C, 35, 40
      lighting systems in, 33
      salaries in, 29
    Class D, 27, 29, 35
      lighting systems in, 33
      salaries in, 29
  expenses of players in, 30-31
  and farm system, 38-39
  lack of future for players in, 25
  life in, 28, 34
  and major leagues, 38-39
  managerial positions in, 37, 39
  pay in, 28
  poor lighting systems for, 33-34
  qualifications for, 21
  qualities necessary for graduation
    from, 39
  total attendance at games of, in
    1947, 1
  transportation for, 31-32
  turnover of personnel in, 34-35
    (*See also* names of leagues and
      clubs in)
Mize, Johnny, 128
Montreal, 50-51
  farm club at, 44, 50
Moore, Al, 132-133
Moore, Cy, 40
Moore, Terry, 125, 189-190
Mound, 8, 14, 61, 66, 68, 115, 139
Movies, as aid to hitters, 199
Murphy, Johnny, 165
Myers, Hy, 119

N

National Joint Rules Committee, 8
National League, 13, 17, 40, 49, 83,
    89, 95, 117, 155, 170, 194
  (*See also* names of clubs in)
National Recreation Association, sur-
    vey by, 1-2
New England League, 30
New York, 2, 5-6
New York Giants, 5-6, 10, 40, 58, 61,
    63, 66-67, 83, 91, 100, 106, 108,

110-111, 116-117, 132, 138, 155, 162-163, 169, 190, 200-201, 203
training school of, 26
New York Yankees, 6, 20, 26, 33, 40, 44, 49, 51-52, 59, 66, 71, 76, 86, 97-98, 104, 113-114, 118, 126, 130, 132, 162-163, 165, 170, 180-182, 190-192, 196, 198, 209
farm teams of, 115
training camp of, 44, 146
Newark, 14, 49
Newark Bears, 115
Night games, 32, 85
arranging schedules for, 52
popularity of, 34, 52
reasons for sideshows preceding, 32-33
receipts from, 34, 52

O

Ocala, Florida, Giants school at, 26
O'Doul, Lefty, 194
O'Farrell, Bob, 111
"One old cat," age of players in, 7
dangers of, 7-8
local rules for, 7
simplicity of, 7
size of diamond for, 8-9
Option rule, and disposition of rookies, 49-50
Ostermueller, Fritz, 166
Ott, Mel, 14, 67, 127, 138, 146, 154
Outfield, 12
shallow vs. deep, 133-134
sunny, 134-135
third basemen in, 93
(*See also* Outfielders)
Outfielders, 13, 55, 75
ability of, to get jump on balls, 128-130
advancement of, 40
avoiding collisions between, 135
backpedaling, 129
bluffing by, 136-137
catching by, 129-131
cooperation among, 135

and defensive plays, 135
and double plays, 134, 136
duties of, 124-129
experience needed by, 126-127
fielding ability of, 124-125, 127-135
and fly balls, 126-127, 129, 135
short, 136-137
and ground balls, 125-126, 130
hitting ability of, 125
infield practice by, 130
and knowledge of batter, 128
muffing by, 124
need of judgment by, 125-126
and pitchers, 124, 126
rules for, 131
signals to, 74, 128
from shortstop, 131
sunglasses for, 134-135
and Texas leaguers, 134-136
throws made by, 131-134
trapping the ball by, 136
(*See also* Fielders)
Owen, Mickey, 114

P

Pacific Coast League, 30-31, 38
Padgett, Don, 14
Page, Joe, 152, 165, 192
Parmelee, Roy, 110-111
Pennants, 37, 49, 108, 138, 201
in 1920, 118
in 1941, 89
strength needed in winning, 97
Pennock, Herb, 203
Pensacola, Florida, Dodgers' school at, 25-26
Percentages, law of, 17-18, 157, 182
Philadelphia Athletics, 49, 97, 128
Philadelphia Phillies, 14, 130, 155, 161, 203
Physical condition, importance of, 18-19
for pitchers, 47
for rookies, 45-47
sacrifices for, 19
Pick-off plays (*see* Plays)

Pickup, 56-57
Pickup nines, 1, 8
Piedmont League, 30
Pinch hitter, 143
  left-handed, 182
Pinelli, Babe, 95
Pioneer League, 29
Pippen, Henry, 189-190
Pirates (see Pittsburgh Pirates)
Pitchers, in amateur baseball, 12-13,
    17-18
  as batters, 62, 91
  batting-practice, 199
  called fifth infielder, 60
  and catchers, 168-169, 179
  chances of, to reach majors, 39-40
  change of pace by, 157, 161, 163
  covering of first base by, 60, 168
  and curves, 155, 157
  definition of, 154
  deliveries by, 166
    timing of, 164
  in double steals, 81
  equipment of, 139, 157
  and extra pitches, 158
  and fast balls, 154-155, 157
  as fielders, 60, 63, 87, 168-169
    of bunts, 168
  made from fielders, 154
  mastery of control by, 39-40, 154-
    155
  need of judgment by, 163
  in "one old cat," 7, 9
  professional, 13, 21, 39
    cooperation of, with first base-
      man, 59-60
    left-handed, 13-14, 167
    major-league, 42-43
    minor-league, 43
    need of agility by, 59
    right-handed, 92, 105, 165-167,
      182
  protection of arm by, 164-165
  in relation to batters, 161-164
  relief, 165, 192
  rookie, 46
  and screwballs, 157

signals to, 74-75
speed of, 139
strategy of, 139, 161-163, 167
style of, 165
warm-up for, 164-165
weaknesses of, 62-63, 91, 115
Pitching procedure, 154-169
Pittsburgh Pirates, 49, 58, 74, 89, 122,
    178
Pivot man, 70-72, 101-102
Players, all-around, 12, 169
  amateur, 1-2, 4-7
    advice to, 11-12, 15, 17-19, 22-27
  earning capacity of, 31
  essentials of, 100
  faults of, 10-11
  left-handed, 12-13
    (See also Batters; Pitchers)
  need for thrift among, 31
  professional, 4-6
    big-league, 21
      financial rewards of, 24
      qualifications for, 23
    minor-league, abilities of, imag-
      ined vs. draft rating, 37
      advice to, 34-35
    professional life of, 9, 24
  right-handed, 12
    (See also Batters; Pitchers)
  room for improvement in, 17
  scarcity of, 26
  similarity to fans, 3
  standards of performance for, 40-
    41
  stories about, 10, 13-14, 18-20, 27,
    42-44, 47, 52, 58-59, 61, 66-67,
    83-84, 130, 146, 153, 167-168,
    194, 202-203
  techniques of, 17, 21
    (See also names of players)
Playground baseball, 1, 11
Plays, off the bag, by first baseman,
    58-59
  close, 55
  cutoff, 132
  double, 60-62, 69-74, 87, 134, 173
  force, 53, 92, 124

at second, 70, 73, 136
at third, 88
hidden-ball, 94-95, 174
hit-and-run, 65, 79, 119
infield, 58
and catcher, 120
pick-off, 64, 179
position, 62
prearranged, 103-104, 118-119
run-down, 107
second-base, 68
squeeze, 89, 149
antidote for, 91
timing of, 8
trap, 78, 136
trick, 94
triple, 173
Polo Grounds, 6, 27, 58, 108, 127, 133, 189
Pony League, 29
Position plays (see Plays)
Priddy, Jerry, 104
Professional-league games, total attendance in 1947, 1
Providence (Rhode Island), 32
Put-outs, 66
by fielders, 129
from foul balls, 116, 124
lost by pitchers, 60
in "one old cat," 7

Q

Quigley, Ernie, 173-174

R

Red Sox (see Boston Red Sox)
Reese, Pee Wee, 86-87, 102
Reiser, Pete, 86, 170, 181-182
Rickey, Branch, 15, 22, 170
Rigney, Johnny, 18-19, 100
Ripley, Bob, 173
Rizzuto, Phil, 27, 74, 86-87, 101-102, 105
Roanoke, Virginia, 138
Robinson, Jackie, 50-51, 170

Robinson, Wilbert, 96, 161, 168
Rolfe, Red, 86, 149, 180-181
Rookies, 132, 146
advice to, 45
and coaches, 191
odds against making team, 48
on first attempt, 49
pressure on, 44-45
publicity for, 44
reports on, 47-48
and slumps, 198
in spring training, 46
Ruel, Muddy, 110
Ruffing, Red, 43, 66-67, 86-87, 169
Rules, 8
Runners (see Base Runners)
Ruth, Babe, 13, 47, 49, 130, 141, 190

S

St. Joseph, Missouri, tryout camp at, 22
St. Louis, 52
St. Louis Browns, 49, 117
St. Louis Cardinals, 6, 13-14, 97, 102, 104, 108, 118, 126, 132, 138, 147, 151, 162, 170, 189-190, 195, 209
St. Petersburg, Yankee training camp at, 44, 146
San Francisco, 11
Boys Club League in, 17
San Francisco Seals, 13, 31, 42-43, 153, 194
San Mateo, California, tryout camp at, 23
Sand-lot baseball, 1, 3, 11, 23, 118
Schacht, Al, 183, 188, 192
Schulte, Johnny, 191-192
Schumacher, Hal, 110-111
Scorer, 173
Scoring, 205-209
by fans, 205, 208-209
fundamentals of, 205-208
methods of, 205
official, 209
Scouting, in amateur baseball, 15
at badly-lighted night games, 33-34

Scouting (*continued*)
  in baseball schools, 25
  as career, 38
  importance of, 27
  and rookies, 47-48
  in tryout camps, 22-24
Screwball, fingering for, 157
Second basemen, 7
  advice to, 75-77, 79
  and attempted steals, 77-79
  cooperation of, with shortstop, 71-79
  duties of, 74-75, 79
    in double steals, 79-82
  fielding by, 68-69
    in double plays, 69-71, 77
  need for judgment by, 77-78
  problems of, 73-74
  right-handed, 68
  tagging runners by, 73
  three plays needed to star as, 68
  throwing ability of, 68, 70
Semipro baseball, 1, 3
  dangers of occasional success in, 21
  fast, 21
  financial returns of, 19-21
  lack of future in, 25
  managers of, 20-21
  as means of learning, 21-22
  as profitable sideline, 21
  qualifications for, 21
  regulars in, 20-21
Senators (*see* Washington Senators)
Sewell, Luke, 110
Shifting, by first basemen, 56-57
Shoes, importance of, 11-12
Shortstops, 12-14, 49
  in bunt play, 63, 103-104
  covering third, 89, 93, 107
  defensive skill of, 97, 103-104
  dependability of, 108
  in double plays, 60-61, 69-71, 102-103, 107-109
  duties of, 98-106
  examples of, 97-98, 108
  as fielder, 97-98, 100-103, 108
  in hit-and-run play, 65

as hitter, 97-98
importance of, 97
and outfielder, 106-107, 131
and pop flies, 106
and relay throws, 93, 101-102, 105-106
requirements of, 97-101, 105
signalling by, 106, 131
and steals, 104-105
in teamwork with pitcher, 103
  with second base, 71-79, 102, 106
throwing power of, 105
Shotton, Burt, 26
Signs, changing of, 184
  given by catcher, 121-122
    by coaches, to batters, 184-186
      to runners, 184, 187-190
  intercepted by runner, 122-123
  simplicity of, 184
  stolen by coaches, 151
Simmons, Al, 146-147
Sinker, 158, 163
Sisler, George, 5, 57
Slaughter, Enos, 126, 153
Sleep, importance of, 19
Slider, 158
  delivery of, 161
Slow ball (*see* Balls)
Sluggers, 12
Slumps, advice for overcoming, 195-204
  blaming pitchers for, 204
  and coaches, 199
  distinguished from bad year, 201-202
  effect of, 195, 198, 200, 202
  emotional progress of, 194-195
  lack of cure for, 194
  mass, 200-201
Smith, Bob, 14
Smith, Sherry, 167
Snyder, Pancho, 10
Socks, need of cleanliness of, 12
Sooner State League, 29
South Atlantic League, 30
Southern Association, 5, 30, 204

Southpaws, 167, 182
  (*See also* Pitchers, left-handed)
Southworth, Billy, 170, 180
Speaker, Tris, 125, 133-134
Speed, of foot, 15, 39
  for shortstops, 98
Spitballer, 161
Sports writers, 60, 67, 141
Sportsman's Park, St. Louis, 87
Squeeze play (*see* Plays)
Stainback, Tuck, 104
Stanky, Eddie, 182
Steals, 104, 119, 174, 181-182
  bluff, 78
  double, 78-80
  on fly balls, 187-188
Stengel, Casey, 31-32, 94, 167, 178
Stephen, Vernon, 145
Stirnweiss, George, 25
Stories about baseball, 4-6, 13-14, 67,
  76-77, 81-82, 86-87, 94-96, 104,
  108, 117-119, 122-123, 126, 129,
  133, 138, 162-163, 169, 173-174,
  180-182, 189-190, 195-197, 204
Stretch, 56-57, 179-180
Strike zone, 147, 154-155, 179
Stripp, Joe, 25
Sun blindness, 87, 127, 134-135
Sunset League, 29

T

Tags, how to make, 81-82, 105, 171
Taylor, Eddie, 173-174
Taylor, Zach, 117-119
Teams, make-up of, in training
  camps, 46
  sure measure of strength of, 97
  (*See also* names of teams)
Terrell, Rick, 120
Terry, Bill, 57, 61, 67, 91, 111, 169,
  200-201
Texas League, 30
Texas leaguers, 75-76, 87, 134-136, 198
Third basemen, 44, 58
  advice to, 91
  alertness of, 85-87, 89, 91

assets of, 85
born vs. made, 83-84
and bunts, 84, 91-96
and catchers, 87
as consistent hitter, 84
cooperation with pitcher, 92-93
and double plays, 88
duties of, 93-94
examples of, 83, 89, 95
as fielders, 84-87
and hidden-ball play, 94-95
  example of, 95-96
need for judgment by, 88-89
and pitchers, 87
and pop flies, 87
protection of foul line by, 85
and shortstop, 85, 93
Thompson, Fresco, 204
Three-bagger, 129
Three-I League, 30
3-6-3 play (*see* Plays, double)
Throws, bad, 57
  to first, 56, 102
  on the fly, 132
  low, 57
  on one hop, 132
  overhand, 101
  pick-off, 64-65
  relay, 93, 102, 105-106, 133
  return, in double play, 60-61
  "into the runner," 53-55
  to second, 55, 61
  sidearm, 101
  snap, 102
  to third, 55
  underhand, by second baseman,
    68-69
  by shortstop, 100-101, 103
Tobacco State League, 29
Toledo, 61, 178
Tools of ignorance, 110
Torgeson, Earl, 44-45
Trainers, and rookies, 45
Training, spring, 45-46, 142
  air travel to, 51
Training camps, 44-45
Travis, Cecil, 26

Index

Traynor, Pie, 58, 83, 89
Trick plays (*see* Plays)
Triple play (*see* Plays)
Tryout camps, 15
    advantages of, 22-23
    instruction at, 22-23
    location of, 22
    major-league, 22-23, 26
    operation of, 22-23
    quality of players in, 23
    of San Francisco Seals, 23
    scouting at, 22-24
Turner, Jim, 40
Two-bagger, 182

U

Umpires, 95, 111, 173-174, 179, 182
Universal appeal of baseball, 2
"Up and at 'em" League (*see* Eastern
    League)

V

Vance, Dazzy, 40, 168, 173-174
vander Meer, Johnny, 19
Vision, as requirement for batters,
    140-141
    corrected by glasses, 141
    examples of, 141

W

Wagner, Honus, 142
Wakefield, Dick, 24
Walker, Dixie, 86, 127
Walters, Bucky, 14, 154
Waner, Paul, 141

Warm-up, need for, 18, 164-165
    example of, 19
Wasdell, Jimmy, 86
Washington Senators, 61, 116, 169,
    183, 190
    baseball school of, 26-27
Week-end baseball, 15, 19
Weintraub, Phil, 163
Western International League, 30
Western League, 30
White Sox (*see* Chicago White Sox)
Williams, Ted, 49, 141, 147, 151-152,
    195
Wilson, Jimmy, 14, 154
Windup, 165-166
World Series, 37
    of 1920, 153
    of 1924, 116
    of 1932, 66-67
    of 1933, 110, 169
    of 1934, 6, 102
    of 1937, 10
    of 1938, 10, 209
    of 1939, 180-181, 187
    of 1941, 86, 114, 171
    of 1942, 13, 104, 126, 162
    of 1943, 118
    of 1946, 51, 151-152, 195
    of 1947, 23, 115, 152, 162, 170, 181-
    182, 192

Y

Yankee Stadium, 32-33, 66, 98, 127,
    200
Yankees (*see* New York Yankees)
York, Rudy, 62
Youngs, Ross, 196